DIPTYCH BEFORE DYING

DIPTYCH BEFORE DYING
a memory novel
§
THOMAS McGONIGLE

Tough Poets Press
Arlington, Massachusetts

Copyright © 2020, 2025 by Thomas McGonigle.
All rights reserved.

Front cover photo by Thomas McGonigle.
Back cover photo by Anna Saar.

The novel originally appeared as *Диптих Преди Умиране*
in the Bulgarian literary magazine *Съвременник* (*Contemporary*).

ISBN 979-8-218-62856-7

Tough Poets Press
Arlington, Massachusetts 02476
U.S.A.

www.toughpoets.com

For Anna

The Left Panel:
To Newfoundland

My father and I went to Newfoundland in the summer of 1973.

§

In the morning Dad had been up before me. An empty beer can on the dining room table. He had smoked a couple of cigarettes. He had changed out of his pajamas and gone back to sleep in his day clothes.

[This is a transcription from that lousy source, reality.]

§

I never met a person who knew him as a young man or even from the time he had met my mother in New York as the country was getting ready to be taken up by World War Two. He is a solitary figure who exists in some pictures in a photo album where he is among people. He is only a photographic representation that when I die the ability to identify him will disappear as my children will have very little interest as by way of their mother they do have grandparents who they knew and to whose funeral they will have gone, though neither of those people have a belief in such ceremonies.

Both of the children have been to my parents' grave on Long Island. For a few years when they were children Anna and I would take them along on Good Friday when we drove out to Long Island, went to the cemetery, brushed away the leaves and planted a couple of flower bulbs in front of the small tombstone and then later go to a diner near Patchogue, drive by the house where I had lived as a child, drove out on the Mascot Dock and usually stopped at a shopping mall on the way back to the city where they were delivered to their mother who lives five streets away from where I am typing this.

§

I heard him snoring. His toothless mouth was open. He clenched a light blanket to his body. He lay in the bed where his wife, my mother had died seven months before.

His dream would be burying the miniature poodle that *had to be put to sleep.* **He took the newspaper-wrapped body out to Sheepshead Bay and buried it in the sand, down deep where the fresh water began to run, he said. The vet had taped the eyes shut and bound the lower jaw to snout with buff colored twine. As the parcel lay in the puddle at the bottom of the hole he thought he detected movement. He ripped it open and put his hand inside. He pulled it out covered with fleas.**

§

Dad, come on, you got to get up. It's time to go. We have a lot of driving to do.
I don't want to go. Your mother can't come with us.
She'd want you to go. Have you packed the rest of your things?
I don't want to pack.
I've packed most of your stuff. See if there is anything missing.
I don't care.

I'll check, don't worry. Get your razor.
To cut my throat.
You can't cut your throat with that.
You think so.
He goes from the bedroom to the kitchen and I hear a can of beer pop.
I have most of the stuff in the car. You gotta help a little. You do want to go?
No.
I pack his fishing pole and equipment box. He drinks the beer.
You want one? He asks. It's cold.
As I am drinking the beer he brings the razor and soap brush in a little plastic bag.
We are off. Ice chest loaded with beer. 9W to the Thruway north from Saugerties.
Dad sleeps in the backseat, wakes up drinks a can of beer, smokes a cigarette, goes back to sleep.

§

The New York City radio stations fade out. Above Albany we stopped before crossing into Vermont so Dad could have a cup of coffee from a machine in the gas station.
I was here once with your mother in Vermont. The car broke down. It was just before the war.
Didn't that car break down on your honeymoon?
Yes, in Virginia. It didn't when we went to visit that wife of yours in Virginia. How is she?
Okay, she lives in the city now.
Good for her. In Virginia, yes, we almost made it to North Carolina. That is where we wanted to go. I wanted to play golf. I had been there with fellows from work. But this was another time. Your

mother and I drove up to Vermont, to see the leaves changing or something. Your mother liked to do things like that. I don't know. We couldn't understand what people were saying. We had a nice time even though the car broke down. Not like that time in the Catskills when they thought we were Jews, do you remember that? I loved Marion, your mother. She was such a good woman.

O, Dad, please.

But I did, Tom, I loved her very much and she loved me. I'd have done anything for her.

You can't do anything for her now. Maybe have a good time.

How can I have a good time without your mother?

He gave me his glasses and went back to sleep, cupped the side of his head in his hand and slept.

Sentences: He could not look at me too long as he knew I held him responsible

I held myself responsible in some way for her death.

She lived out her life for other people, she said.

She never really cared for herself, more selfish than any of us because she wanted us to be left with the knowledge—you did so little for me, I gave up my life for you, I couldn't even read the magazines, there was always too much dust . . . I always put all of you before myself.

§

We were off to Canada, just the two of us: me and the old man. I resisted the expression, the old man: the old man got me this, the old man got me that, the old man was drunk last night, the old man is quite a guy.

§

In the hospital she seemed like a pink stain on the white linen. Go away, she said. Go away. I don't want to see you . . . is my hair messed up . . . my fingers are so ugly . . . how can anyone . . . your father . . .

§

All the time I had been with Dad since Mom died I kept saying to myself: I have nothing to say. What can I say?

§

He sent me to Italy and Bulgaria a month ago. I had been in Sofia on May 24 for the day of the language.

§

Across Vermont and stopping at a small motel and cabins within sight of Mt. Washington.

New Hampshire was where Carol Lynley came from in RETURN TO PEYTON PLACE. She had written a novel and gone to New York City and come back home to meet the townspeople.

§

There had been floods, the guy in the motel said, keeps people away. Back from the road were big houses at the end of drives. The unabridged Webster's dictionary is on a stand in the library of the house. The mountain was green going to black into a darkening sky behind a sign selling souvenirs.

§

Dad and I sat at a little table in front of the cabin drinking beer the owner had brought for us. Each of the six bottles was on its own little napkin.

Tom, I'm going to sleep early. Okay? You don't want me to go out with you, do you?

No, it's okay. I might drive into the town, look around, see what's going on.

So go on then, I don't want to keep you.

§

A concert was breaking up at the pavilion in the village park. I wrote but do not know what I meant: the first bar was vinyl. I saw a woman with blue hair who had a toothpick at the corner of her mouth. I recorded this song lyric:

> I'm just an hour of time
> And a six pack away
> From forgetting you.

Right here: stopped.

§

Do I recount a conversation in another bar, part of a big resort, where I went, go into a crowd and being told it was a party for the employees and asking if I could stay, seems like the people are having fun, and being asked what I was doing and saying I was going to Newfoundland with my father?

Distraction in November we gathered at my mother's hospital bed. She could not eat. She did not want to eat. Don't let the food go to waste. I've never had Thanksgiving dinner out. The next Sunday I had to cook a turkey. Dad took a sip of Mogen David wine. She was just in for tests, really. Maybe she could try to eat some cranberry sauce and some of the white meat. It hurt too much. When she got home . . . yes, she had gotten home. Everything was going to be okay. It had always been like that. The Fanellis next door left her cut flowers in a vase with a statue of the Infant of Prague attached to it. [*gathered* = a linguistic attempt to avoid reality]

§

I heard a bottle cap come off a beer. Dad was shaving and drinking. How do you feel, he asks.
Fine.
You got in late, I heard you.
So . . .

You can drive he told me and I asked if he could help me and he said, maybe.
The intake of the smoke and then the sip of beer.

§

We didn't talk during the rest of the day. Drove into the Maine. Didn't see anyone around and not a lot of traffic. Forest on either side of the road. An occasional church on a hillside and tombstones around it.
Stopped at a crossroads store and got two six-packs and a bag of ice. He didn't want an infrared ham sandwich even though they had the hot mustard he liked.
Across the border at St. Stephen. Just waved us through. On to St. John. Union Jacks in the breeze. Easy to love England with an ocean between. To the Loyalist City.

§

Another day—as is always sometimes said.

§

Benedict Arnold tried to make a go of this imitation Glasgow, from my experience. We had a drink in a nice bar.
I'm tired, he says. Let's find a place for the night and you can come back later if you want.
But you slept all the way
I'm not as young as you are.
A little less beer.
Let's find a place
The motel with a newspaper.

HUSBAND KILLS WIFE AND THREE LOVERS IN ST. JOHN MOTEL ROOM

Do you need anything, Dad?
I'll be okay. Go into the city and have a nice time.

§

I transcribe my first version of what happened next in town: There are no good times in this city. At night the bar where we had been won't let you in unless you have a tuxedo on. Walk around and find a bar. A big room with a couple of old men sitting in chairs watching the television. An ante-room to a flop house. I walk across the room and there is a smaller carpeted room. Again a television but at least there are some women to look at.
You can't sit here. The waiter is standing next to me. He has a beard and jeans on.
Why?
You have to have a woman with you to sit here.
What?
It's the law. Now no trouble now, you know the law.
Where can I sit?
Outside with the men.

§

Found in a plastic bar [*plastic*, a slang word whose meaning is obscure but which it seems everyone had a definition for it] near the motel.
   GANGLAND SHOOT OUT
   THREE WOMEN DIE
     TEN YEAR OLD BOY HELD

Drink a little of that protestant Moosehead beer. Two bottles make you sick and swear to give up the drink for an hour of faithful resolve.

§

Dad was sleeping. I have **FOR MEN ONLY** to read and a new novel *ALL THE LONELY YEARS* and from St. John we went to Moncton to Sydney in Nova Scotia for the ferry to Port aux Basques, Newfoundland.

§

However, in the morning: slice of well-done bacon, scrambled eggs, coffee, no orange juice, just two eggs sunny side up, whole wheat toast with butter, a glass of milk
The history museum:
men go down to the seas in ships
drown
My brother, Dad says, was a ship's radio operator and president of the Wireless Operator's Association.
Yeah. I remember that funeral and knowing he drank himself to death and I saw kids tearing apart the mourning wreaths at the grave a few over to collect the metal frames, a sort of deposit on each one.

I'll drive a bit, Dad says.
Up a long hill.
A far river drinking a bottle of Pepsi.
I'll have a 7UP, Dad says.

§

A cabin outside Moncton.
Lot of French people around here.
Let's go to the movies.
CLASS OF '44
 the Dad dies
 kid sees the old man's shoes in the closet
 his empty eye-glasses case
 I don't even know what he looked like
 his girl was waiting for him
 silly happy ending . . .
It was pretty accurate, Dad says. Made me sad. That's the way it was.
 We have a drink in the bar in the mall where we saw the movie.

 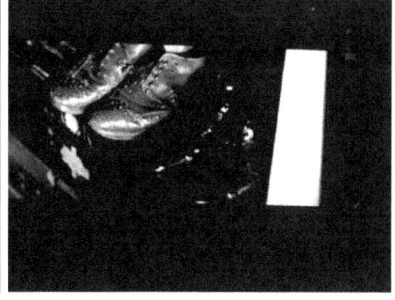

§

We stop at another bar off the road to the motel. Rock being read from the music sheets in front of the musicians. Dad smiles at the waitresses. We drink cognac and beer. Dad has a cognac over the rocks. Likes the place
 The waitresses smile at the old man. He must have some sort of secret.
 See maybe the emptiness in the heart, my heart, a sewer for a

heart.

Dad has a love of some sort.

I went out and threw up in the bushes. Dad was worried, should I do the driving? No, I'll be okay. I sat in the car and he went back into the bar. Came back in an hour. I liked that place. Good to get out but your mother wouldn't have liked that place. Something like the bowling alley in Times Square that the CANCO used to use on Monday nights . . . a long time ago,

So you're set for Newfoundland, he says and I say, I am.

§

A MAN'S DESIRE NOT TO HAVE CHILDREN IS A DESIRE TO SEEK EXTINCTION

On Sunday in Sydney they convert the bars into churches. We drank in the room, took showers and slept for the next day when we could take the ferry to Newfoundland. The day was long with him saying: I want to send a postcard to Deirdre.

Downstairs they must have them.

Could you get me a couple?

You got two legs. I'm not a servant the way Mom was.

She wasn't a servant. She knew how to do so many things. I was good to your mother.

I remember.

No, you don't. Before you were born. She understood me.

That's what you've always said. She understood you right into her own grave.

That's not true.

Shut up, you're drunk.

You drink as much as I do.

Shut up. I wanted to punch him in the face, break his glasses into his brown eyes, let the brown float like shit in his blood.

§

Then the *whatifs* . . . why did I stop at the kiosk in Sofia, why did I put my hand through a door window in Mattituck, why did I go back to Sofia from Istanbul, why did I drive away from Hollins?

§

Did we go to sleep or pass out?

§

There was a good feeling waiting to drive on to the ferry. People seemed different. Raw hands, I saw, something I never notice, usually, some tourists but most people just seemed to be that, people going home or going to visit the home place.

Dad seems happy, buys a paper from the kid and tells him to keep the change from the dollar . . . I knew he had delivered newspapers when he was a kid in Brooklyn . . .

what I knew of his actual life in Brooklyn wouldn't make up a paragraph.

§

The car was down in the hold of the great ferry sailing from Sydney to Port aux Basques, Newfoundland: I like saying the word Newfoundland . . . the *o* gets dropped out it seems or at least off my tongue.

Found the bar. A red and white plastic semicircle. On the arc small round tables with four chairs about each with an ashtray in the center of the table and four Moosehead beermats. The waiters have been drinking all afternoon before we board. They've loosened their ties and their silvered serving trays are stained from the previous sailing. A red napkin covers the little pile of coins on each of their trays.

Dad and I sit next to this couple. **CAN YOU SEE WHO THEY ARE OR IS THIS DESCRIPTION MORE OF ME, THEN?** He and she of this couple have the look of people who hated the smell of babies and milkshakes, well, they've probably had the children but now free of them they were lonely and happy and a scotch was in front of each of them and I knew they would talk to us because they could talk without a child pissing into her ear and he saying, they are children after all.

And this other couple comes in. She has long red hair and is slightly heavy. Her eyes are green as are the trousers he is wearing. He seems just out of the Marines, heavy hairy arms, a long full beard and hair like a patriarch in a Jewish village in Poland though his voice is American mid-western . . . no, he's probably a nice guy and I am a louse for making all of this up.

We sat, Dad and I sat, comfortable in a place where the drink was a necessity and not a vice, where the hand held with comfort a pint glass of Guinness even though there was no Guinness to be had and I thought of McDaid's in Dublin where I was drinking late Sunday afternoon and a lad next to me puked across the floor, went to the toilet, not too steadily, coming back asked for his glass to be freshened and it was for he was not in such a bad way and was a quiet one, to be sure.

And the essential quote . . .

> Everyone enjoys a good story. At six we clamor for stories at bedtime; at sixteen we call for them around the campfire; at sixty we count on them to pass our armchair evenings.
> —ADVENTURES IN READING

§

I want to be in love.

I turn to ask Jill if she would like a drink. She had been called Jill by the man.

I'll have an orange juice. [what follows is the sort of stuff that got cut] If I had one more drink I'd give you my Mom's bra size.

She's not kidding, the man said.

Of course I'm not. I know you'd just love to know my mom's bra size so you could put me down. [this phrase is possibly the remaining actual voice of Jill]

So, you'll have an orange juice?

Yes, with some vodka in it.

[a conversation had been here but was removed for too obvious reasons]

During the serving of the drinks Dad took a scotch from the couple to his left and said his wife at died in December.

And this is my son, Thomas.

I shook hands with Mr. and Mrs. Casey from Toronto.

We're not originally from Toronto. We're Newfies.

What's that?

From Newfoundland. Left there 20 years ago with my childhood sweetheart (he pats Mrs. Casey on the back of her hand). Got tired of the snow and the potatoes and the smell of paper-making.

Now that the children are grown up I go home to visit. We go home to visit my sister and her mother, while we can.

My father was from Ireland, my father said.

And so was mine, said Mr. Casey. County Cork.

Mine was County Donegal. Tom went to Donegal once. Almost married a girl from there, I think. (Dad, don't) Didn't like the place though. I wish he had liked it. Instead he married a foreign girl from Bulgaria of all places. I wish he had married an Irish girl. I'd like to be able to go to Ireland.

Dad, shall we go to Ireland for Christmas?

Will you make the arrangements?

Yes, if it works out in Mexico.

Yes, Mexico. We're going to Mexico, Dad says, to meet my daughter after this place. It would be nice to go to Ireland. My father never said much about Ireland.

Wasn't he very young when he left Ireland?

Not young. He never said anything about Ireland. Ireland was a place to die in, he said once, I remember. He hated Ireland. Everybody called him the happy Mick but he hated the place and enrolled me in the Ancient Order of Hibernians. This was as close to Ireland he wanted anyone to go.

Why did you let me go to Ireland for university?

You wanted to go.

God, Tom, you've a great old man. My old man threw me out of his house the first time I came home drunk. I was thirteen, I think. We were still living in Newfoundland at the time.

Ron raised his glass to Dad. That's why I ended up in the Marines, the American marines of all things. I'm like all the Newfies on this boat, these poor bastards, hating the fucking place.

Cheers.

You should say cheers a hundred times. [more conversation removed]

I'm sorry, Jill.
You must not be sorry.
Nicest girl I know, Ron says kissing her on the forehead and when the glasses came we raised them.

§

Tom you and your dad ought to go up to and see the sunset. It's real pretty. The one thing that's pretty in this place.
Dad, you coming up on deck?
No, I'll sit here. It'll be cold up there.
No, it isn't. You'll like it.
I like it here. Go on will you and leave me alone.

> [what comes next strikes me as something it would be
> impossible to believe though upon reflection there is a
> truth in it and while I am pretty sure Tom did not have such words
> in his head as he stood on the deck]

§

The sun is flattened out on the horizon. A gold tongue In profile. Hair of Lois in the summer, but I never saw her in the summer, only in the winter cold. Lois was in New York and Dad's words, leave me alone. He was always saying that. I wanted to capture: **leave me alone**.

§

Bring on the darkness.
As I started down the stairs Jill was walking up and asked, walk me around the deck.

[a conversation removed]
Jill has left the deck. I didn't want her to leave. We have not commented on the wooden floor of the deck, the tiny pockets or rust waiting to be scraped and repainted. The toll of weather.

§

Dad was drunk by now and the usual . . . being embarrassed as he . . . but it was too chilly on the deck, too alone, so back down to the bar and Dad was sitting where I had left him. He seemed happy. Why was he happy? Ron and Jill were off at a table by themselves. Mrs. Casey was talking in a voice much louder than before, these kids, I don't understand them.

Nothing to understand, Dad says. Just close your ears and eventually they get tired of hearing themselves talk. I learned that living with my mother back in Brooklyn and all my sisters and the nieces. They just get tired.

My son is studying in Toronto. To him everything I do is wrong. Either it's not traditionally right or I'm supposed to be against the revolution.

§

I don't read the newspapers anymore, Dad says. I used to buy the old *Journal American* when I commuted out to Patchogue. But that was for the comics and the Money Word game. Tom, here used to think he was going to win a million dollars and fly off to some castle and have his own army and wear the Kaiser's own golden helmet. You know I used to see the men off at the Brooklyn docks during World War One. I played the flute.

You don't seem that old, Mr. Casey said.

I'll be 67 the day after my son's birthday in October. I forget how old he's gonna be.

29, Dad.

Yes. 29. 1944. The war was terrible.

You were in service?

No.

I was in the desert, Mr. Casey says. Left Newfoundland and ended up in the damn desert, but Mrs. Casey waited for me to come home. I don't know. I wasn't much of a catch. We had a hard time of it.

That's what I don't understand about the kids today, says Mrs. Casey. They've been given everything and still they're not happy.

We are happy.

I don't really believe you, excuse me, Mr. Casey says. Maybe you are but most of them young people . . . Our son is not very happy and that's why he studies the past and the future. Doesn't see much in the here and now. Just likes to talk to people he says.

§

I am waiting for Dad to talk about the American Can Company. About making c-ration cans. Having to go from one end of the country to the other, from Florida to Maine. That's what I had to do. There was something wrong with my heart so they didn't call me up.

It was not talked about: what he did during the war and even now when thought about the other Dads never talked about the war, it was just something they all went to, came back and didn't talk about.

§

I have listened to myself. Almost believed it. My home in the middle of an ash heap and yes, Marion I am still waiting, is the television loud enough, can you hear Julie Andrews singing, she liked Julie Andrews and she was on television the night before. I could hear her teeth cracking pieces of ice, that's all she could eat . . .

I resented her being sick, being in the hospital, I wanted to be with Lois in the city, not there with the white coated nuns, crucifixes . . . . . . or when she was home again for the final weeks which I did not know as the final weeks . . . even found fake poetry: sad voice of tears

> She did not ask for me
> Long ago
> I was a disappointment.
> So many times
> You are just so unhappy,
> she said to me.

§

[a memory that got inserted in a random fashion] Not knowing Mom was going to die, Deirdre had bought a Christmas tree and the day after the funeral she put it in front of the church adding to the decorations around the outdoor Nativity scene. We didn't feel like decorating the tree . . . Christmas was over forever for my sister.

Dad's lips are thin, clenched, pulled inward. There is some sort of electricity between him and the Caseys. They will not have to see each other on the morrow.

Tom, it's a coincidence. Mr. Casey's name is William and Mrs. Casey's name is Alice. A small world, if you ask me. I've always said it, a small world. Alice was a good sister though she married a Protestant. She raised her children to be good Catholics, you remember? Ernest. That was her husband's name. He always bought a new Cadillac every year. William was my brother. He went around the world before he was 17. I don't know how many times after that. He was a radio operator on this yacht you see for Burne-Lowe. He was a rich man until he lost his money in the Great Depression. He jumped out a window, my brother said . . . smashed up on the street he was.

We were living in Wisconsin when my sister Alice died and we couldn't go to the funeral. Deirdre had just come back from the Peace Corps in Tunisia, you know? Tom was there too, we sent them a telegram. He had just left his wife

No, Dad I went to Columbia. Lilia had her course to finish at Hollins.

Yes, I guess, well, he had a place and Deirdre stayed with him

She didn't like the cockroaches and the shower in the place.

She told your mother and me she thought it was luxury after Tunisia.

I guess it must have been.

They went to the funeral together. I liked Alice.

§

Somewhere else I was alive, maybe. This is fiction. Amid, my mother's blood, the warm jelly placenta her blood flowing into me through me . . . the blood that would kill her 29 years later in my life.

Dad telephoned. Your mother died. I went to see Steve Miller down at the place where he was making Xerox copies on Warren street and keeping a bed in the storage room as he was saving his money to buy a Ford 1968 Mustang.

We went to the Blarney Stone (it's still there under a different name and has been there for all these years). They still had the prices in big red numbers up behind where the bartenders stood. A beer mug was being filled with dollars and quarters by the customers for the holidays. We had a couple of beers: Miller's beer like his last name. I was a creature of habit.

§

I just sat there jealous of every single person. Ron being to war, Jill being with him, the Caseys, Dad and here the son who watches porn movies and wanted to rescue the girls from the bad guys so he can be bad to them.

Is that secret enough? In a toilet in Sofia, by mistake in the woman's part the toilet filled with bloody strips of cotton, pee mixed with the blood, that's what it's all about, I guess.

§

The ferry has docked. The bar looked exhausted. Something it cannot be, I knew, but the words got thought and I would have said them.

I woke Dad. No one thought it strange people just lay down on the banquette along the wall . . .

His mouth was open a little. The false teeth yellow, a spot of drool on his two day old beard now.

We've arrived in Newfoundland.

We've got to go down to the car.

I don't want to.

We have to.

Your mother's not with us.

She is in a way. Let's go.

§

He cocks his baseball cap to the side. I walk behind him to make sure he doesn't go over backwards. While in the car waiting to drive off we have a bottle of Moosehead between us. They let you buy it as you are leaving the bar.

In the car next to us I hear French. We give them an extra bottle of beer.

You off to St. Pierre, I ask.

Oui.

Have you been there before?

No.

We'll see you there.

Oui.

Waves to Ron, to Jill, the Caseys, the French people.

§

Out of the ship, down into blackness beyond the floodlit lot and then more just blackness . . . really cheap with the lighting . . . No stars, no moon, chilly, no signs after the terminal. Rear red lights disappear . . . just drive a bit and then a hotel.

WELCOME TO PORT AUX BASQUES

I'll go in and see if they have a room.

No, I have some reservations that haven't shown yet but they are old customers, can't disappoint them. A Playboy calendar behind him. May flesh, old May flesh, should have turned the page.

No room, Dad. I'll drive until I get tired and then pull off the road and sleep for a while. We have to get to Corner Brook.

What's that?

The next town on the map.

How far?

Couple hundred miles.

Do you want me to drive?

It's okay. I'll drive and then we'll sleep.

§

The headlights reveal nothing but the road and a white line down the middle of its spine. Black shapes which must be houses come out of the gray and disappear to the sides. My hands feel like pliers on the steering wheel. I don't want to die. A closed gas station, maybe the next one we can sleep at. I slow down, a car passes beeping it's horn. Two lit cigarettes sit in the front seat, that's all I can see. I slow down again looking at the rear view mirror. Crawl along the side of the highway. A driveway. Back the car into it.

Tom, have we stopped, Dad says. Is something the matter?

I'm too tired. I'm falling asleep. I'm just backing into a driveway.

You sure it's safe?

I think so.

Slowly back and then suddenly we are at a crazy angle Dad and I looking UP through the windshield at what would be the sky.

What happened?

Wait a minute, Dad.

I open the door and there is no ground under the door. The back wheel seems embedded in soft earth.

O my God, Tommy, how are we gonna get out of here?

Take it easy ... I'm shaking ... how should I know ... I did it ... take it easy ... too much to drink ... always knew the damn guardian angel wasn't on the job ... I'm heartily sorry ... Dad, I'll get out and push ... when I say go give it the gas ... there is a deep gully ... maybe 20, 25 feet down along the side of the drive ... my feet sink in the soft earth ... I trip ... the palms of my hands are cut by the gravel ... I try to push at the car ... the smell of rubber ... smoke ... Dad it's no use ... he gets out of the car ... I don't know how he did that ... his bald head in the now sudden light of a passing car

... Tom, why did we come here? ... why did we stop here? ... I was tired ... let's try to push together ... It's no use ... Tom, get in the car and give it the gas when I say ... I'll push ... I have to get you out of here that's what fathers are ... you can't Dad ... I'll try ... nothing happens ... more smell of rubber ... O, Tommy, I've dirtied myself ... I've dirtied my pants ... the smell of whiskey ... beer ... diarrhea ...

Get out of the pants and find your clean ones. You packed them didn't you?

I can find them

So get out of your pants ... I'll find them.

Dad's legs are withered vines twisted sticks.

I'm so embarrassed, he says.

It could happen to anyone ... we'll have to get a tow truck.

Dad sits on the ground near the car with the new pants on. Dad. Daddy.

I wave as the cars pass by ... some slow down and go by like I would while others stop and say nothing and go on.

A priest taking some boys home stops ... he's a young guy, a kids' friend. Dad says he doesn't feel well ... the priest and the boys talk to each other ... he comes back and says we'll go get this boy's Dad's tow truck and pull you out.

Dad and I sit there and they do come back.

They really did.

Pull the car out just like that and don't ask questions.

Can I give you some money for your trouble and time, Father, Dad asks.

No, we just help each other in Newfoundland.

But I'd like to.

Send it to Catholic Charities in Port Aux Basques. Have a safe journey.

I don't like to owe things to people, Dad says I'll send him something when we get home.

§

Drive on.
The priest said there was a gas station a couple of miles down the road. A bar across the road was still open.
We went in, veterans of a hard fight. Ordered up two beers each and two for the road.
Can we sleep in the parking lot? No room in the inn.
Sure, why not.
The beer was good and I slept in the front seat and Dad slept in the back seat and we drank all the beer and in the morning the sun came through the misted up windows.
My breath on the chilly July air. Mountains all about: skulls upon which trees grow. The parking lot was pebbled and rutted. Nature would take it back. A stream on the far side of the road lead away somewhere as a deer was drinking and then suddenly alert and away.

§

Dad, are you awake?
I'm always awake. I was awake when your mother wanted me. She might wake up at any moment and need me in the night. I never slept all those months.
Shall we get some breakfast?
I don't feel like eating.
What about coffee and an egg?
A cup of coffee.

§

I wiped the dew from the windshield and drove the highway. An empty land. I do not like people very much. The trees have been harvested. The lakes look naked with no trees about them. Stone and rock, a Japanese stone garden built by a nation of giants.

§

Dad looked and said nothing I had him sitting on the edge of the bed calling the doctor, the priest, the judge across the road. Cold, the cold spreading cross the sheets, lapping at his legs swimming up his ribcage.

§

HISTORY LESSON. Newfoundland, first seen as I knew by Cabot and before him the Vikings and even the Irish were said to have been here. They left no skeletons, only a few marks on stone.

§

Ate breakfast in a gas station . . . the restaurant was part of the station, oil and steel: the wrenches lying in their compartmentalized chests, the girl smiles when she takes our money.
Have a good journey.
I hope so. She probably didn't think twice about my answer. People were left to themselves. Dad sat and smoked and I drove. I was a failure. He was a failure. We both knew this, really knew this. We drove or I drove rather. What to do with knowing this?

> O you might think its goofy
> But the man in the moon is a Newfie
> O you might think it's goofy

But the Man in the Moon is a Newfie

The words repeated themselves over and over again in my dry mouth. All we wanted now was Corner Brook.

§

A paper mill and a Holiday Inn. Dad had his credit card for Holiday Inn. You know what you are going to get. Not like going to see an old friend you haven't seen in ten years. Eccentricity is a lonely voyage. Maybe I should be like Michelangelo and stick my hand up the ass of a dead person and puke when I touch the back of its teeth.

§

Dad and I drove against the coldness of the road. No cheap tourist word photographs of what we saw.

§

In Corner Brook, Dad went to the bar and I went to the movies. I saw *Borsolino* and *A New Leaf*. What a combination, you might say.

Dad sat in the bar of the motel talking about his wife, my mother. He loved her so much, you know, don't you, what can I do?

I climbed the hump of stone in the center of Corner Brook, get a view of the place and found a weather-beaten twig, carved by Bosch of the devil's head, I thought, really.

When I got back to the motel and the bar I asked Dad, Let's go for a drive.

I drove out of the city and turning a sharp corner Dad slammed his head into the sun visor and cut his brow. HE was like a little kid. He bled into his handkerchief. HE was very alone. I saw his blood. His blood. Mom always took care of him when he was sick and now he only had me.

What's the matter? It's only a little cut.

It hurts. My head hurts so. Hurts.

We sat in a large empty room of a bar.

We have strippers here at night if you want to come along, the guy behind the bar said.

Tom you should come back and have a good time. My head hurts too much. I don't feel well.

§

I did go back there. It was like the go-go place up on the highway between Appleton and Menasha . . . in 1966, in Wisconsin: see beautiful INGA. I wanted to talk to INGA . . . take her and this girl in Corner Brook away from this and just dump me, she is thinking, look at you, take me away from what and to where: you got to be joking, mate. She just likes to show off her tits, not down there, you aren't allowed to show off down there, from Vancouver to Newfoundland.

Come along gents. Time. Finish your drinks. Gents. No trouble. Now. Gents. Time.

Long into the night of Molson's Canadians . . .

A couple of Canadians for the road.

Under the moon, yes, I remember the moon and looking down to some sort of body of water and logs glistened, waiting to be turned into paper or something or other.

§

Dad was not in the bar. He went up to his room a couple of minutes ago. You just missed him.

He missed Mom's death, I think I know and he knows I know this. In spite of being there all the time, he missed it.

Dad was in the bathtub peeing on himself.

What the fuck are you doing?

Sleeping.

You've wet yourself.

No, I'm sleeping.

Come on. Get out of there. You'll get sick, catch a cold. Then what would I do? We better go back to New York.

I don't care.

The acid smell of urine. My father. Dad. Why. Daddy. Dad. He slept as he fell into the bed. I washed the water around in the tub. Urine has a hot smell. Dad, why. Okay, I pee into hotel sinks but at least I get the fly down first.

Must have thought the urine would be dry by the morning, so why worry. What's the big deal?

§

Dad snores I went to drink. The bartender says you have a good old man. He left this here by mistake. He gave me the five dollar bill and I used it to buy some beers.

I went upstairs and passed out and awoke finding Dad sitting by the window saying, when are we getting on the road?

After a swim. Do you want a swim, Dad?

No, I'll go get a coffee.

I swam. Breasts, cunts, eyes, blonde hair filled the holes of my head. I was alone. What if one of them said, hello?

§

Dad and I drove to Gander. On our drive around Newfoundland, you can't go across the place.

In Gander, once, stopped on my way the first time to Europe. An airport cut into the night.

Now rows of one-story buildings and houses built about an airport. Dad was tired. He sleeps in the Holiday Inn. I drove around looking for moose steak. It was out of season. In season you get so tired of the stuff you long for just an ordinary hamburger. Roads going out of town disappeared into trees. The movie theatre was only open on weekends. Like a lot of places the kids leave as soon as they can and then come back when they can't enjoy the place anymore, a guy say says in a bar.

Had a beer someplace and got a case of Molson's for the car. Ice is free in the Holiday Inn. The bar of the motel was the insides of an old airplane.

Did you see a bald man in here before?

Yeah, he went up to his room, I guess. He related to you?

My father.

Take care of him. Something's bothering him.

He hadn't taken his coat off. His hat was still on. He had put his glasses on the table next to the bed. He'd pissed in his pants.

Dad, wake up, you've pissed in your pants. Why do you have to do this. Just like you used do it to Mom. You killed her with this stuff, don't you know it?

He didn't say anything. Just moved in his sleep. At least he hadn't broken his glasses. Maybe he should have. Give him something to really complain about.

You have to get out of your pants.

I don't want to. I don't care, so why should you care.

You have to.

I turned him over on is back and unbuckled his belt. Thought of which woman.

Come on lift your ass up. I pulled the pants off and put them in a paper sack. They also stank of shit. He was asleep again.

I drove out to Gander airport. He'd sleep it off and maybe in the morning be good. That was the phrase: Be good. Can't you be good? He would not remember. If he did he would know why I would not forget. We travel knowing all of this, I think, maybe.

The airport was larger than remembered, done up in blonde wood and endless Canadian cheerfulness which I could never match. The shopgirls sold gossip to each other. From Gander one can fly to Europe twice a week, away from the filth of the new world. Pain. Common pain, left in pain, with hope still on their lips, lips. No one to talk to. So I drove from Gander to sit eventually on the balcony of the hotel bar and drank as the sun went away.

§

Dad and I stayed at the Holiday Inn in Clarenville, Newfoundland. A sprawling sort of place at the center from which the spokes of rooms radiated: a large bar or pub as the sign announced: SIT AWHILE A WHILE AWHILE ...

I didn't want to go on. Here we could decide whether to go on to Fortune and the islands or to go to St. John's or go back. I don't remember why and how and why it was decided to go back the way we came.

I know Dad didn't want to drive around the village. He liked staying in the motel. He ate his lunch there. He sat in the bar. He made friends with a doctor from St. John's. He didn't see any reason for traveling. He didn't care what we did. I didn't want to go to St. Pierre Island. The idea of going was better than the going. They spoke French there. I didn't want to go with him.

I decided we would go back the way we had come. Dad agreed. He wanted to get back to Saugerties. Why'd we go traveling in the first place? What had been the point? You didn't ask that question when she was alive. I didn't have a reason to. Don't wreck the car with your drinking. I won't.

Clarenville, a village with a shopping center: parking lot not paved. Walked about the shops. Wanted to buy toilet paper, soap powder, a large box of corn flakes, a half-gallon of milk, a jar of allspice and if they had fresh ginger?

Look as if I were new in town and just stocking up.

Had a beer in a bar that they hadn't finished building yet. No rush, the bartender says. We don't get many people in here. Not much reason to come into the village. People rush by staying at the motel up on the highway.

You staying around here?

No, just for a few days.

If you did you'd go crazy.

Maybe not.

I don't know. I thought I would at first . . . when we moved here . . . I guess if you think you'll go crazy you don't.

I don't know.

A gray airy bar from which I could see the harbor. I thought of Pula. Always thinking of someplace else. I would kill Dad but he was my father. Lonely as a finger of Turgenev's, as sad as the roses about the grave of Bach in St. Thomas Kirche in Leipzig. [while there is an arbitrary pretense to this . . .]

§

Dad was drinking whiskey with Dr. whatshisname from St. John's. If you get your son to drive up into St. John's be sure to call me. If I'm not there my nurse will take the message. I'd like to show you and your son the morgue. I think it would do you good. You'd realize how young you are. Ireland might be a nice place for you to visit. You could see why your mother and father left. Where did you say your father came from?

Donegal.

You get there and you'll know why he left. They probably had no choice in the matter anyway if I know my history. And I do. I can show you the morgue. Usually they don't permit it but in your case.

I don't like hospitals, Dad says.

Neither do I and I work there of course. In the morgue you don't have to act and put on a show. No one is going to smile at you with their pathetic eyes.

I don't know.

I hope I'll be seeing you and you'll be still using your legs. Make your son come along,

He has a mind of his own.

He's too young to have one of those.

Have a drink for the road?

In St. John's.

Here.

No, I've got to be going.

Go to hell.

That's always a possibility. Neither one of us will know for sure. St. John's?

I'll see. Tommy, you'll have a beer. Get me one too.

Yes, Dad.

The doctor left. He didn't say goodbye to me. We hadn't been introduced. I just listened. Dad went to the bathroom. I got a second bottle of beer.

Red tablecloth. Ashtray piled up. Empty glasses, bottles: a new family shared activity with the edge of what it did to the body... see if he or she could survive. The knee of my jeans was going but better the knee than a split up the backside.

Dad had been talking with the doctor. The doctor had been

talking with Dad. A doctor. How in a couple of hours had they known so much about each other that the doctor could suggest a visit to the morgue?

I sat in the green bar in town. The guy behind the bar was different. I could see the waves were low and gentle upon the shore as if waiting for a storm. Went back to the motel.

§

[I know this not from experience but from a wish for it to be here]

That night Dad was thinking about being a guard at the St. George Hotel in Brooklyn. This had been during the war to pay for my brother's birth and for his death since he didn't live.

The hotel is seedy, Mr. Casey had said on the ferry. How did he know that? Memories went seedy. The gun rusted, broke into pieces even as he carried it on his hip. She had been the one to kiss him in the evening when he got home. It was always very late. Working two jobs for her. He was the one who cared, Mom said.

§

Next day, Ron and Jill showed up on their way back to North Dakota. An argument with his father. He can die alone and bury himself, Ron said. Lumber wasn't any cheaper in Newfoundland and the best had been cut and shipped a long time ago. Now there was only scenery left. North Dakota is like Newfoundland without all the stumps of barren harvested woodlands.

We have to go back to his father, Jill said. We had a few too many drinks at the bay there and then it hit Ron he couldn't leave the old man like. Just can't do that. You're stuck with him and he's stuck with you.

They left. Dad asks why didn't you marry a nice American girl?

But no, you break your mother's heart and mine. You see Ron and Jill. Ordinary people.

I guess so.

I'm having another. I lost the wallet with the pictures of you and your sister and the two ducks you had in Patchogue, you remember them, Wacky and Lucky, I don't know what happened to them.

I went to the room alone and drank from a bottle of Screech.

§

In the morning Dad ordered two pan-fried steaks and french fries and cold really cold bottles of beer.

Tom, I don't want to go to those islands. I am tired of traveling.

We have to go to Mexico.

I've lost my wallet. Mom might need us. Your mother wants us.

We're going back to Saugerties.

§

[partial poetic aside]

Finally, on the road again. To be in Corner Brook by night. Words are swallowed. Januarius is the name of this guy who wants to talk about the man who steals smiles and the story of the man who is talking about mouth jobs behind the Pan Am building. [How to date the reference] And the Brady Hotel. Melinda has a room there.

Finally.

All you can do is do what you can do.

§

Dad's head hurts again in Corner Brook. He has no interest in drinking. He slept. I climbed up the mountain again and again found a piece of weathered wood in the shape of an incomplete crucifix: much too symbolic to be believed. Both pieces of memory got lost somewhere along the line.

Hilda would be waiting in Saugerties.

The wallet and photographs were found.

Dad posed for a photograph that did not come out.

Picture taking was not part of this journey.

§

In Moncton we stayed in the same cabin again. Like returning home. A two-car head-on crash on the road right in front of the cabin. Blood on shattered glass. Smell of rubber and a dead dog moving into a final shape.

A night drive to a hill indicated as a site and experience not to be missed. Car parked on the road. Engine turned off. A *mysterious* force pulled the car up the hill backwards.

§

The quick descent through Maine and across Massachusetts, this time.

In the papers a card for SUNSET MOTEL. Auburn. Maine. On the back:
SAUNA BATHS, POOL
IN ROOM COFFEE
Going into the dark sauna as I remembered the red front of the outside of the motel. I sat in the heat for a few minutes and aware of being alone back to the room where Dad was sleeping.

As one looks at the postcards the isolation of the motel and the aura of sheer loneliness are evident. The sunbathing woman of course confirms this: the woman possibly being the daughter of the owner. The power lines suspended from the poles across the front view of the motel.

§

Home again to the house and the mail collected by the neighbor.

Dad sat in his chair. The jacket still on. A bottle of beer. She did not call him.

I planned for Mexico

Hilda would drive passed the house in her old Chevy, one of the springs in the back was gone. She was looking for the car so she could call from the candy store opposite the Exchange Hotel to meet me in Woodstock where I first met her late at night drinking in The Pub, this old blonde woman who was drinking Guinness because it was a natural beer . . .

THE END

These sentences were removed from the book but if this was a DVD (the fascination of Deleted Scenes) . . .

Corner Brook:

I telephoned Steve Miller in Muncie, Indiana.
What are you doing, Steve?
Drinking and waiting to jerk off.
So what else is new?
Gary's in jail for drunk driving.
What else is new?
My father has a new mistress. He told Mom tonight at dinner
When are you coming back to New York?
After I get the money to buy a Mustang.
Have you ever watched your father pee on himself? I'm sick here in Newfoundland. It's very lonely.
It's the same in Muncie. Gary says they have the best heroin in the world in Muncie. They don't kid around here. You see I'm using the language of the place.

It's good to talk to you, Steve, only Harvard grad I know.
No kidding.
Well . . .
Bullshit, McGonigle, you become a killer when you're drunk. Watch out.
I'm always doing that. Any women out there in Muncie?
Millions and all married.
Shall I come visit you?
Bring enough beer to pay for this call.
I'll try.
You only got one father, Tom. They don't grow on trees.
Yeah.
Be serious. I know what you're going through. It's the same here.
It's always the same.
He's your old man. Is he asleep?
Yeah.
So go and have a drink. Tomorrow might be different.
You're not angry I called?
Why should I be? What are friends for? My father will shit a brick when he gets a bill for a call from Newfoundland.
I'm on my way to the bar.
Good thing.
See you in a couple of months. My sister, me and my father are going to Mexico City after this.
I'll see you in New York.
I'll probably see you in Muncie, first.
Take care.
Say hello to Gary when he gets out of jail.
Lurch: when the trousers split for some reason in sixth grade I was afraid people could see the white of my underpants. I did the trousers up with the belt in some complicated way so you couldn't

see the white of the underpants, thinking myself a wounded soldier.

I was so afraid.

I don't know why.

They would know something about me.

I didn't know what they would know about me.

It was something from Boy Scout camp, I think.

Deer was something to be on the lookout for. Deer were very scarce. Deer was the cry. DEER DEER DEER. A group of boys would run after any boy who was alone. DEER. Grab him and pull him the ground. Take down his pants, turn him over and bare his bottom to the sun. His silken balls. DEER. DEER. They grabbed me. Head against dirt. Yank my belt off. Held up my ass to the sun. Pour Coke into the crack. It burns. I cannot cry. The dirt sticks to my skin. I pull up my pants. I am a man. I don't want people to see me.

The Right Panel:
To Mexico City

[The left panel of the diptych has partially deteriorated while the right one has elements from the left which might as a result be a little allusive but upon a closer reading this is only apparent and not reality.]

There has to be a missing photograph and the one I am missing is of my father entering a cantina behind the Hotel Del Prado sometime in the afternoon between the 7th and the 14th of August, 197—. His hand is upon the top of one of the swinging doors.

Inside the cantina we sat on the bench with our backs to the street and I had been up to the bar for *duo cerveza*, paying for the beers with a bill as I didn't know what they cost. The guys looking at us had seen men like my father and I: he old with a slight tremble to his hand, smoking one Pall Mall after another and me the son putting up with but glad for the beer.

In a sack next to me I had a bottle of Mescal with the worm at the bottom.

We are not in the bar of the Del Prado where my father sat for much of the week we were in Mexico City.

Not a remembered word.

Not even an attempt though once I did write out in accumulated pages of conversation what I was to have remembered from this sitting in the cantina: conversations going on and on and while possibly some tiny basis in either experience, remembered experience or needful invention, I now know them to be false in a way back then I was unable to understand and my delusion held fast for too many years, but those years have only added to the crummy falsity of their existence so I can only list the titles I gave to the various "books" containing some of these now remains that did not see their way on to a shelf in printed form:

Long Night of the Twentieth Century. A Comedy.
The Wounded Seasons
Hearts of the Dead
Broken Mouth
Mating Games of the Octopi
Delusions of Decency.

We had three beers each. There was the one to get settled, the one now knowing the price I was able to leave the exact change for on the bar top and then a third for the road, as in our family the most savored: one for the road—done with the visit, see you soon but not too soon . . .

> And again, Ford's discreet camera distance, and his behavioral doodling on the margins of the scenario, create epic feelings without bombast or pretension.
> —THE JOHN FORD MYSTERY by Andrew Sarris

I bought two roundtrip tickets on Mexican Airlines from New York City to Mexico City and I must have also reserved a room at a hotel the person in the travel agency recommended.

August was not a busy time, might have been said, and there might be some rain during the week we were to be there 7 to 14 August. This date I discovered in my sister's handwriting on the back of one of the photographs from this journey.

According to a date calculator we were there from Tuesday to Tuesday.

I found a carbon copy of a note to the travel agent:

> Enclosed is my father's check in the amount of $582.00 as full payment for seven nights at the Del

Prado Hotel in Mexico City and for the Roundtrip air far via Aero México leaving New York on 7 August.

Later in the month I was to go down to a writer's retreat or colony or something like that at the Virginia Center for the Arts.

I seem to think a car met us at the airport in Mexico City since neither my father nor I read or spoke Spanish. I had for my guide some writings by Jack Kerouac and D.H. Lawrence. I must have looked at Octavio Paz's *Labyrinth of Solitude*, the title appealing to me, as it would have for one in my situation. I knew a street in Mexico City: San Juan Letran. I knew no other and would use it as the point about which to circle from after leaving the Hotel Del Prado.

The hotel was destroyed—I know now—by an earthquake and replaced by a Hilton, but surely I am not the only person who is incapable of placing a Hilton Hotel into my head with our leaving the Hotel Del Prado so as to walk to San Juan Letran—a street name discovered on a page by Jack Kerouac—which now comes complete with a subway stop and possibly the news it no longer really exists since swallowed up by another name or who knows what . . . but I was to walk along there in both daylight and night time, always wishing not to be alone, but alone I was and knowing no other streets I used it as a point about which to circle from after leaving the hotel.

In my walking around I found a bar in an enclosed patio of what had once been a convent on the other side of the *Alameda* from the hotel and to the left of where I would be then sitting was the *Palacio de Bellas Artes*. I sat at a table and wrote in a book. I was always writing in a book.

There is something both pathetic and despicable about such an activity as I look at the person there sitting in August, 1973, but that is also a way to hold it at a distance though I do wonder if it is still, as surely it is since I am not given to speaking in voices or hearing voices, if now that person is the same person sitting here pressing these keys on an electronic device at 46 East First Street, Apartment 3D in Manhattan, New York, New York, USA.

There had not been such places on our way to and about Newfoundland, that is for sure.

By the time I was in Mexico City with my father I had thought myself bereft of any sort of companionship or being possessed of friends. I did know I would be going to Virginia to stay at a retreat for which I had been referenced to by Annie Dillard and Hannah Green.

I had other places to sit in Mexico City: a bar on the top of a hotel of a building overlooking the central plaza across from the cathedral. My father had no interest in going into churches or cathedrals as they were something like hospitals that he knew as places you went to die in: a belief he still held, as is said, in this day, shake of the head.

My sister came, on her own, from California to Mexico City and would be returning separately to New York after a further journey to Yucatan. She must have joined us when we—as what remained of the family—went to this bar as the photographs show us with the background of the cathedral down there . . .

We had walked there from the Hotel Del Prado, for the taking of a stroll. Never in our lives had we taken a stroll.

At the same moment . . . as I am talking with Jose in the organic pizza place on First Avenue, around the corner from here, right now . . . to be faithful to the illusion that I have spent all these years both observing and writing about this time in Mexico City: of course I am not having you on as this is the actual present moment—yet the organic pizza place has been replaced by an ordinary pizza place reminding us that at any moment it might be our last as I never when I began imagined that the pizza place would become an ordinary pizza place since the organic pizza place had a guy from Acapulco making the pizza and that was to be the obvious link since he had not been to Mexico City except to change planes when he flew to New York City to stay with his sister who had made way for him . . . : the three of us were driven out to Teotihuacan in a car arranged at the hotel, a large black American car from maybe the early '50s as it seemed like the Dodge my father had until we go a new car in say about 1960 or so . . . with the very high front seat and us sitting as children in the back seat, only the back of their heads visible . . . there was a driver who did not really speak English . . . we knew we were going to Teotihuacan and the Cathedral of Our Lady of Guadalupe and he would be taking us to a place where we could get silver stuff very cheaply, from someone he knew . . . I can't reproduce his poor English or our inability to speak a word of Spanish beyond *si*.

The weather like much of that week was cloudy and while it didn't rain until we were back in the city center, we seemed to feel threatened, not being prepared and who knows what could happen.

I did not stare at the people shuffling along on their knees across the plaza in front of the cathedral. I no longer wore a cloth scapular for the Immaculate Conception medal . . . all of that from so long ago . . . in the portico of the cathedral, crutches and other medical devises hanging from the ceilings and the walls . . . I felt the absence of my belief ever so visible in those knees moving over the stone . . . I was thirsty and had to pee . . . my sister had been sent relics and little statues when she had polio and while she was recovering . . . Mass cards with her intention inscribed by relatives and colleagues of our father at the Can Company . . . her being singled out by the disease and why had it caught her and not me, or why me and not him? But I never imagined that question for my sister.

When we came back from swimming at the shorefront in Patchogue she collapsed and was taken to the hospital by ambulance across the island to Port Jefferson and I was waiting for Dad to come from the city. Back then.

I should go back to Bulgaria but I am also in the back of the big black Dodge from late '40s early '50s complete with running board going out to Teotihuacan those pyramids outside Mexico City in August 1973.
My father drinking from a bottle of beer is sitting up front with the driver . . . I didn't bring a bottle with me and my sister is just sitting next to me as we did in the early '50s returning to Patchogue from visiting Brooklyn relatives. My mother's cigarette glows brighter and the dims in the dark. She is yelling something at him for going so fast and the car hits something by the side of the road.
Later I realize that . . . but I knew nothing, right then, except the noise and the cigarette getting very bright and then dimming.

Somehow and I do not know how it is but our mother is now driving the car within months of that coming back from the city.

Of course Dad was drunk. Everybody was drunk in those days, gets said now . . .

To be aware of: do you remember the way it is . . .

So these words fall like stones of some sort . . . can I call into existence *someone who will be able to construe these words?*

Dad doesn't share the bottle of beer. He never has after those times, back then, the last sip of a glass . . .

Where are we going? He suddenly asks.

To look at the pyramids.

We are not in Egypt.

The Aztecs had pyramids. We are going to look at them. I think you can climb the biggest one.

I am not going to climb anything.

(Did this conversation take place?)

For a moment a glance away from the three of us in that car heading for and from Teotihuacan.

I had found two places to go off to and **to write**. The grandness of those two words is hard to read as I type this now forty years later.

That is what I said I was doing. I don't know if Dad heard what I was saying as he always asked me when I later saw him in the hotel bar, where did you go?

He never asked me what I was doing, what I was writing about. I did send him an article I had published in *The Village Voice* entitled "A Son's Father's Day." He told me all the fellers at work were really surprised to see your article. I write in the article I was drinking myself to death and in fact after it appeared I no longer felt very involved with Columbia . . . if I could even begin . . .

In these two places that I found: one, across the *Alemeda* in what I was told was an abandoned convent I sit at a table off to the side of an enclosed patio . . . the other place was in a hotel down the street from the hotel and then you turned left as if to walk into the *zona roza* . . . you walked through a lobby and suddenly a large room with some sort of booths about the sides and back, a fountain of some sort in the middle under a skylight. I sat at a table down in the center of the room.

I write at the pages and then: what I was doing was writing the name Melinda, Lois, Melinda, Lois and hoping to call then into existence as if words could produce a living creature in the chair to my right or left, not across the table as that would seem: some sort of interrogation.

end of this distraction.

But unable to return to that car on our way to or back from . . . So.

In the week following our return from Mexico City I went down to Wavertree Farm in Virginia to write.

I kept a small journal with these sentences:

The only faith and enduring love affair is the one with death.

HE SLAMMED MY EVISCERATED CORPSE

AGAINST THE SCHOOL HOUSE WALL MY SKULL OPENED SCRAPED CLEAN ALREADY.

And a quote from Artaud: This unusable body made out of meat and crazy sperm.

EARLIER, in another book I found I had written and which I transcribed while down at the farm: So starting another journal so many before, so many sad pages from which I have learned nothing.

I did not add anything and from which I will learn nothing. A person learns nothing from what he has written himself. It is always, finally, only for the other that writing is done.

I did not know that and I probably could still find myself disbelieving what I have just written.

For a long time I have known of the reader that Mandelstam insisted upon as being both in the next room as I am here at the desk and alive a hundred years from now. If the words cannot hold those two destinations they have failed, utterly failed and . . .

So then as now I did not think about it. I was unable to place myself anywhere but on the bed in which I imagined my death about to take place and once again Melinda had not come to see me.

This thought held me in both places and has visited me even, so many years later, as I sit here on East First Street, Melinda will not walk into this room, she will not even think to call *out of the blue* but . . .

Here the reader is taken back to Mexico City, across the Almeda, across from the Hotel Del Prado in the abandoned convent.

. . . a short very Indian woman was—every time I was there—mopping the floor with the slowest possible motions and either I did not spend that much time at each of the occasions I was there working on my writing . . . she never seemed to finish her mopping and I was forced to mumble some sort of excuse for crossing her path on the way to as I would have been saying to myself, take a leak, use the bathroom, use the men's room . . .

I did not grow as the popular sentiment wanted me to do. I am not a plant.

I knew one word *cerveza* and did not need to know any others: I was an American in Mexico City. I could be nothing else. I was not about to become instantly fluent in Spanish so why bother. Be that as it may. Only a few more days.

And then when Mary Ann was there finally we went to the Latin American Tower and for the first time I ordered *surf and turf* which came in quotation marks. I do not remember if the menu was bilingual as there was no point in having menus in only Spanish or only in English. I must have pointed to the "surf and turf" as some sort of lobster and steak appeared eventually. Dad ordered a hamburger that he ate at with knife and fork. He had a few mouthfuls and then stopped. Mary Ann must have talked of going to Yucatan and we would be seeing her in New York in a couple of weeks. She must have been taking a bus as she was used to such travel from her years in Tunisia—a time there in the Peace Corps—about which she never talked and it was for the same reason, I suppose, why I did not talk about my years in Ireland or in Bulgaria.

What is the point of talking about foreign travel? You were away and now you are back. I had been away and then she had been away. Postcards were sent upon arriving in foreign places and postcards were sent when leaving these foreign places, trying to send them early enough so that the cards appear before you do.

From the tower it was supposed to be the view to be seen but at night all you see are lines of intersecting lights . . . many of them moving and disappearing at the horizon. Not being natives of Mexico City we could not as I imagine the Mexicans were pointing to where they lived or where they were staying with an authority so evident in their extended finger pointing arms.

Dad's head began to nod toward sleep and when Mary Ann poked him he said louder than . . . Marion I'll be right there.

I saw the people at the table besides us look in our direction. They were Mexican and turned quickly away. If they had been American there would have been smiles bordering on smirks, though what was being known would remain . . . while the Mexicans saw what they were not really interested in.

The Mexicans we had come in contact with had been friendly enough: smiles and head noddings and the sounds of course were agreeable though, for all I know they were cursing while smiling, but I doubt it for to go to that extreme did not seem necessary and would involve too much of an effort which in turn would be telling me or us, you have been seen by *the natives.*

I am well aware the expression the natives can be construed in a less than positive way but it so accurately reveals the gap I felt at least at this moment and in all the other moments of our week in Mexico City: the natives did not become individuals with names, tiny bits of personal lived history as a result of the minutes we were in each other's presence. If there had been a Pedro or Juan or Maria might we have spent years going back to and reliving that week in Mexico City by the simple act of saying, remember when Pedro said to you . . . or Maria handed you . . .

Never did we talk about any one individual with a name attached to that person when later . . . though it might have been because the visit was sealed behind what happened, five days after my father and I returned from Mexico City, on 19 August, a Sunday afternoon, how long such a period of time can seem—the hours of a Sunday afternoon—though at first I thought it was particular to small towns Upstate, but I have felt this in New Jersey and in

Patchogue and here on East First Street in Manhattan, this dreary expanse of time paired to the moment in a parking lot up in Saugerties, on the west side of 9W coming from the south toward the town . . .

Dad said he felt sick to his stomach a little when we came out of the elevator from the restaurant. Mary Ann said she felt tired and would go back to the hotel with him. It was not far away and maybe the air would do him good. I was going to go walking along San Juan Letran.

I do not know how I knew of that street, I should be writing right now, and how at the end of it or near the end of it was a collection of bars and late at night musicians who had been wandering through the bars of the city came here to continue playing.

Yet I do know and I hesitate to admit to having read a book back then, wouldn't it have been better to just go along on San Juan Letran as if I had stepped on to the face of the moon, yet the now crummy wrinkled, paper browning and cracking, cover faded, illustration of a disheveled woman smoking sitting on a bed *what are you going to do now?* on the smaller than usual Avon paperback of *Tristessa* by Jack Kerouac shoves itself to mind so I had first read the street name **San Juan Letran** there and since it was so close by and I had walked by it on my other walks about the city—not very adventurous to be sure and I kept the little map the hotel gave us mostly in my back pocket and only looked at it when I thought no one could see me.

This morning here in New York I walked through Astor Place and a little kid bumped into me, ever so gently and quickly backed away. I noticed his mother was looking at a map and I could hear what sounded like one of the Scandinavian languages but I for one cannot hear the differences between Swedish, Norwegian, Danish, not to mention Finnish or Icelandic just to be . . . but I was not aware of having bumped into anyone in that week in Mexico City. I had put my money in my front pocket of the jeans. I had no jacket to wear and it was mostly too warm for one . . . though that Sunday we did see a bullfight in the rain and there was an excursion to the anthropology museum and then to the other places in Chapultepec Park . . .

But there had been no human contact in any of these places. One was to avoid it, I had been told or think I remember being told by David Vanderlip who had been to Mexico, the first of people I knew who had been to Mexico . . .

On Juarez just down from the hotel there was a bookstore and a bank next to it and walking back and forth in front of the bank were young men with pistols at their hips, low slung as if they were modeling for westerns . . . unlike the police or guards in the US . . . the pistols angled out for the possibility of a quick draw . . . I was aware of the crowd on the sidewalk and was afraid of being pushed and being pushed into one of the gunslingers . . . One of the guards had the heel of his hand on the top of the handle of his pistol and there was no safety strap holding the revolver in place. In Istanbul the police walked about with holsters at the hip but with no pistol under the button-down flap and at the same time the patrolling soldiers carried automatic rifles but no ammunition clip was visible . . . someone told me at certain times the soldiers did carry loaded rifles and the police actually had automatic pistols in their holsters.

All of which is to say I had been in foreign places and saw something of them.

If I had a camera I would not take pictures of people.

Up in the park was a museum and a room or rooms, I forget how many, were there to show how Maximilian had lived and of course I thought of Trieste on the way to Bulgaria the first time and not going to Miramare Castle as I did not approve of such visits: you can see perfectly well the sea, the Adriatic sea, from the hostel what you can see from that castle . . . where the widow dragged out her life and further along I know now Rilke had been at Duino . . . and I was going to take the boat to Pula having met an American on his way to see the Cedars of Lebanon: seems a time long ago, so remote from the moment . . .

Mexico resided in a drunk under the volcano and going from the halls of Montezuma and even now in a note a friend says she and her family never really went to Mexico as they were afraid of Montezuma's revenge . . . and every person who has been to Mexico talks of being sick . . . the end of *On the Road* takes place in Sal's sickened bowels, and of course Manet is always executing Maximilian . . . the Mexican camera has a love affair with public executions . . . and to get away to Mexico, to go on the run, to be there and find as Marlon Brando does in *One-Eyed Jacks* again with yourself and the money running out so do you go back or go on and walk into your death?

Along on San Juan Letran most of the shops were closed and even darker than the night if that is possible. No family scenes and nearly empty places with one man watching a television high up on a shelf in the green painted light.

Walking along with not a snowball's chance in hell that someone was going to call my name . . . and eventually a square opened and while here were a few large places, brightly lit and with many people coming and going, owning as it were the place it seemed to me.

I wanted to be able to go into one of the smaller places, with the gang of us, have a beer but stopped, stopped by nothing more than: how can I go in, get the attention of the bartender and no one came up to me with stretched hand and people walked with great purpose and I slunk away, as if I had done something wrong.

I walked around in the shadows behind the back of the guys playing guitars, their big hats—sombreros I guess you can call them—slung on their back and a few of the older men had on these broad hats that one is to think as typical—though on the wide avenues I hadn't seen them . . . of course I didn't have a clue as to what they were singing or was it all staged for the drunken groups entering and leaving the bars . . .

Neither rejecting nor rejected I walked back the shuttered street and found my way to the Del Prado.

Dad was not in the bar of the hotel. The barman was at the table and with a bottle of *cerveza*. I signed the check and left some sort of change on the table.

Nothing came to mind. People having a good time. Not even being bumped into. No altercations as the newspapers would have been reporting in the late hours with our foreign visitors who talked of the good times they were having and the more to come as they got to know our friendly people.

I had left my pen up in the room. I could feel the map in my back pocket and I felt it was plastered across my eyes as a sort of necessary blindfold. The execution squad does not want to look into your eyes. They are simple men only doing what is required of them. The ink would stain my skin.

You have such sad eyes, she had said and they avoid me too much. I can't stand a man whose eyes avoid me. A man is supposed to pretend the woman he is with is all of that half of human kind. You are always looking away.

I would walk out to the lobby turn for the elevator and ascend to the brightly lit room as Dad had fallen asleep on the bed with his jacket still on and his shoes still on though they were not on the bed. This time I did not disturb him. He had taken his glasses off and placed them on the night table. I could not avoid looking at his shoes. In Moncton we had gone to the movies and saw *Class of '44*. We had never gone to the movies since drive-in movies back in Patchogue.

This terrible going back into a dead time though we are always trying to convince ourselves that time neither lives nor dies.

O, yeah, the shoes. In the movie, the boy sees the shoes on the floor of the closet of his dead father. Empty shoes, shoes that had been lived in: the past tense saying everything, of course: get out the violins and not the von Webern programmed violins.

On the flight back from Mexico City, Dad began talking to the woman who was sitting next to him. I was at the window and he was to my right and all through the flight he was talking to this woman across the aisle. I never heard him say the words, *my wife*. It's possible he did say those words as I heard him say, this here is my son next to me. He had a long evening it seems. I could see her nodding her head and he did show me as we were driving Upstate the name, the address and a telephone number she had given him.

Since I was not awake for much of the flight I don't know if he gave her his address and telephone number. During the flight he only had two cans of beer and probably looked to see if American Can had manufactured the can. I am sure he told the woman he was retired from the company, the American Can Company, and was living Upstate. We had moved back from Wisconsin where the company had sent me.

That woman was from Westchester, he said, as we were driving, her son was coming to meet her at the airport. She was saying Westchester is almost next door to Upstate. People have strange ideas about geography. I didn't tell her about your mother. I know she was going to tell me about her husband. There was a white line where she used to have a ring on the finger of her left hand. They had to cut the ring off your mother's finger. She couldn't get it off anymore.

The woman asked me where we had gone and I told her Mexico City and she asked me if we had gone anywhere else and I said your sister had gone on to Yucatan and then she started telling me about all the places she had been to and all the things she saw. I didn't really, you don't have to, really listen as people just want to talk about where they have been . . . they don't care if you care about it, they just like to talk. It doesn't bother me as I learned to close my ears, what am I supposed to say, there's nothing to say, really and you know that, don't you? She was a nice woman, I guess, she has a lot of pep but I just don't understand what all the going about is all about, you know what I mean. Your mother used to say she would go traveling when she used up all the places in New York State.

I am not sure of all of this as we had—I forget now how we got from Kennedy to Upstate, to Saugerties, across the river and Upstate. Dad called it Idlewild as that was the name he knew it by. Good thing I didn't have anything to drink on the plane, I should have, but it was hard enough driving. In 1964 I was saying when I went to Europe the first time in September on my way to Dublin I had flown out of Idlewild and was corrected when in Dublin the following June when someone said no one knows it by that anymore. It is JFK and I had been squeamish about saying the joke of the moment: Aer Lingus, the line of the flying virgins and Cunnilingus was the freight branch or something like that, as we did drive by the sign for Aer Lingus Irish International Airlines, and Dad saying wasn't that how you came back from Dublin that first time? . . . going there by way of Iceland, right, he was saying and Bodkin next door met his wife there who was a nurse in the American airbase hospital . . .

And Dad was suddenly asleep . . . and we are back Upstate and I was still in Mexico City up early in the morning to go along to the huge market behind the cathedral, on the other side of the big public square . . . there was a row of stalls that had arranged on shelves heads of cows, sheep and goats, tongues hanging out . . . another row over caged chickens and caged ducks and . . . in the early morning not many people like myself and I was thirsty and hungry and just kept walking . . . of course there were so many stalls selling fruit, vegetables and all the junk of human life but it was the aisles with the dead and soon to be dead animals . . .

Of course, I thought of Bulgaria that previous spring going with Medy to *halleta* in Sofia and watching the guy clobber the living fish with a large wooden mallet . . . it was the only sort of fish people in Bulgaria would buy if they had to buy fish. No one bought the canned fish if they could avoid it . . .

The constant going back and back and then here again . . . the eyes of some of the cows had been cut out and were in a little pile on a tray at the end of a row of heads. The guy would pick up the cow's head by the ears or rather what was left of the ears and show it to the customer and if there was a nod he would put it down on a big piece of newspaper and then drop it into the held-open string bag.

When a carcass was hanging from its rear legs: lambs or small pigs there was always a little band of dark blood hanging further down from the nostrils.

On the way back to the hotel I went into the House of Tiles as it's called Sanborns and I can spell it out in Spanish from the book Casa de los Azulejos. I pointed to a picture of eggs and something else. The waitress looked at me and went off and in the pause of this sentence I had waited, eaten paid and was back on the street. Just knowing only one thing: I was alone and by now Dad was awake in the hotel and we would be going to the bullfight.

The guy in the hotel tourist office gave us the tickets and said in the summer they try out young bullfighters. It gives them what is it you say, experience for the regular season . . . You can't learn to fight the bull in your head, I'm sure you know this, you can't do it only in the country out there in a village way beyond the city: you have to come into the city eventually, be in the big stadium . . . these are not good seats but they are high up . . . that is the best way to see it for the first time, away from being there too closely, to see why people come to see what they are seeing, up too close it is all personality and something to be written about and make photographs of and you look at the people looking more than they're worth. And you can't understand what they are saying . . . Americans always insist on the best seats in the house . . . you don't want that, I think.

However, did this man: here is the descriptive pause in recollection:—thick brown frames of eye glasses, heavy black hair combed back from the forehead, a broad face, blue suit jacket, white shirt and black tie, neither tall nor short as he never stood all the time I was in the office—the brown envelope with the tickets had been handed across the desk to me, silver ring on the second finger of his right hand with a small green square of stone: enough you might say—begins to talk to me in the office off the waiting room with the faded posters and the broken down over-stuffed leather-covered chairs which in the years developed wounds that had been sewn together, but never healed, he was saying, when he could see my hand was on the sewn wound of the seat of the chair next to the one I was sitting on.

The woman who sews our chairs no longer seems to be coming by the hotel, I can't account for her disappearance as we pay her well and in cash and she did her work quickly with no expectation of something more, I think, but one can't tell people all the time what to do and she was one of those people, maybe as your hand can feel on the wound—the words from a song: *in mortis examine*—that is what your fingers are moving over and I have seen you with your father is it? . . . when you came for the car to see Teotihuacan . . . that is another reason for the seats I found for you and your father as already it is all too close to you and I am sure you feel this as he goes to sleep or if you awaken and see him sleeping, preparing his face, we say here, sleeping, preparing our last face to be remembered, something, maybe the only thing we do not **have** to do, to remember *that*—what we looked like when we were last seen, though they remember and you will remember forever and ever as they say, ever and ever . . . replacing the living with the last memory, with your father you will enjoy going to the bullfight, it is not to my taste but it remains here and it will remain here though I am not in any way . . . sitting up in the heights you will not be targets for the wild ones who like to throw things and as long as your father keeps his hat on he will not be a provocation . . . it is written about in one of the English language books about Mexico that the little boys like using the bald heads of the *gringo* for target practice—I do not know in pursuit of what it is they are training.

Eduardo has come into existence.

We never say Eddie or Ed like the Americans do in their constant intimacy, their constant drawing the wagon train into a circle, even if only on the basis of a person's first name, Eduardo was saying, once the tickets for the bullfight had been pushed across the glass topped desk, I had a friend who called me Ed. He had heard the name in an American movie he had seen and liked the sound of it, as it was foreign and we each saw the other as a visitor from some other place: I wanted to come from Russia and sometimes I wanted to come from China, don't ask me why, while my friend wanted to come from the US of A. He liked saying that: the US of A. He liked the sloppiness of the Americans and told me the formality of our people will be the death of our people: as you can see we were both experts before our time. My friend said we were so formal we had a code worked out for the different coughs a person could utter for a multitude of purposes . . . and I'd ask him where his English originated and he would look at me as if I was talking about the dark side of moon or some other place at which point in an impossible to believe change of topic he asked if I was . . . and I will complete that sentence for you as it gives the wrong impression.

You are to take a taxi, Eduardo says, as a pause came after his sentence. I notice as his hands moved about on the desk, moving pages from here to there and then straightening the little pile that a blue and white paperback book moved into view and then disappeared but not before I had seen the title *The Clothes of a Dead Priest*. The author's name was unfamiliar to me yet it seemed close in spelling to John Currier or it could have been John Carrier.

I did not ask Eduardo about the book as I thought his revealing it was all he had wanted to do, though I could not understand what he had wanted to tell me by showing this book.

A taxi, from the front of the hotel and the driver will know where to leave you for the entrance these tickets will allow you to enter. I doubt the stadium will be very crowded since it is summertime but those attending will be there for the most honorable of reasons: the tickets are cheaper, they can really feel superior to these toreadors, they will be encouraging of the young and sometimes the comedy is of the highest order since it is wrapped in blood and death, even if everyone involved is not of the first rank. And you should feel no compassion for any of it: this is the hardest aspect of going to such a spectacle, it is a moment away from the usual, a necessary turning from so as to turn back.

Sea deep thoughts are to be kept away from yourself and you should enjoy wondering when the boy with the beer will be up to where you are seating yourselves . . . these trivial details are finally more productive, if one must be vulgar about such a matter. There will be an element of winnowing to be witnessed: the last days of the aged horses, the bulls that in some way are defective, not being fully worthy of being killed by a master . . . and while the bull hardly has much of a chance and the toreador runs his risks, there is always an unbalance . . . the superficial wounds inflicted on the bull, don't ask anyone their opinion of any of this as this is your advantage of not speaking Spanish . . . the banalities of protest and explanation.

Trust yourself to what your own eyes see and be able to ask your father what he sees and I do hope he will be able to find words for what he sees as such a spectacle is more ably described by he who is closer to his own final moment but I fear I might be intruding upon your own wish to be closer to the end of the story, am I not right?

I had been listening to Eduardo's voice and while it is probably impossible for a reader to believe I could have remembered this conversation at this great remove—as the old books would have it—I have to say Eduardo is here as close to me as the skin on my fingers is to the bones it covers. Though there is no way I can claim to be an anatomist and use the resulting authority to plead my case: yes, I did remember what Eduardo had been saying though I am willing to grant some of my memory might be frazzled by the passage of the something or other, but that is neither explanation nor defense of the veracity of my transcription of his sentences.

If it rains and it is likely to rain on such a Sunday, a boy will appear with clear plastic rain capes and the fight will go on no matter the weather . . . as in football matches: the weather contributes its share to the struggle, unlike baseball that is so easily defeated by the weather, baseball the constant humiliation of its players by the whims of the weather through which the football player and those in the impervious struggle with the bull labor for a conclusion must to be achieved no matter.

I dislike the poverty of our languages to describe this weather my friend in Arizona calls *the monsoons*, admitting in his choice of this word, a failure of linguistic imagination, a poverty in need of bringing over from the far east this word, *monsoon*, but no matter, a Sunday outing for you and your father different from what you are used to—I am sure—back at home as it is for me also—a time to rest, to sleep away the gloom that always descends with a fierce swipe of a mental scalpel that cuts always after two o'clock on a Sunday afternoon any strength we might have as we, the two of us know, the week will again be here and this foolish day of rest and never asking: rest for what?

It makes me nostalgic, Eduardo says, leaning back against the high back of his chair which seemed to shrink him to only his voice though of course a man, really, a man who had found these tickets for the bullfight and who was not going away and would be at the hotel in the morning and was saying do look in.

Would it be possible to imagine I handed Eduardo this photograph which I had taken during the intermission when these young men wheeled out this platform with a large Pepsi Cola bottle wobbling and after a few minutes in the rain they found as they tried to return the platform that the wheels had become stuck in the surface of the ring and additional workers were called into both push and pull the platform from the ring so the rest of the program could begin?

There would be no need for the evidence, Eduardo was saying, I do not always believe what I see as I am sure you are also skeptical of those who retreat and that is the necessary military word for this defection from the art of the tongue, if I may wax on before your scorn melts me to a puddle. You have seen something we would not have seen and for that I can only thank you—though of what significance can it have as already it is a form of ancient history, due only to evaporate as the color of your photograph will fade or as in some cases burst into a sort of golden obliterating stain?

Another boy brought around bottles of beer and a Pepsi for my sister who was also with us, but while she inhabits some of my memories of this week, she claims only a place at the edges as she went about on her own to her destinations and with her plans to go further into Mexico while Dad and I returned north to New York.

She went to a museum of the doll and was much taken by a doll-inhabited hospital room, a doll assembly displaying the regional traditional costumes from the different provinces of Mexico, a display of dolls dressed in what she took to be the American Dream and another representing the glamour of Paris and a sort of two compartments displaying to the left the birth of a beautiful set of twins and to the right the funeral of those twins separated now into the two centuries: the Nineteenth and the Twentieth.

The rain was refreshing, she said, as she had spent two years in Tunisia teaching school and it rarely rained in Sfax. It would be a mistake to ascribe to her the second part of that sentence as she never ever mentioned being in Tunisia, as that was her own world and she did not want to share it with me and the confusion in what listeners might make of our own individual journeys. It was bad enough I had met her once in Scotland when she went for the first time to Europe on a mistaken, as she later admitted, tour of England and Scotland. She was traveling with other young men and women who for the most part did not know why they were going where they were going but had been sent by parents who wanted them to experience foreign places in the safest possible way.

However all of that was long ago—though not really—but it seemed to be and that is what counted now. She would push on to the Yucatan on the day we flew back to The City and see the pyramids there which were said to be more impressive than what we had seen on the outskirts of Mexico City.

In the fine rain we sat to either side of our father. Eduardo had said something about coming from a very large family and being lost in the middle of so many brothers and sisters he often thought of his father as some sort of distant monarch who, he was sure, only vaguely knew his name and where Eduardo was in the midst of the family. The oldest and the youngest are always known by such a father. Who comes in between is a member of the reserve crew or team waiting for his or her moment but that moment would always be wrapped in sadness and in his case never happened as his father was killed by a truck while crossing the street. Eduardo and his brothers and sisters were parceled out among uncles on both sides of the family.

A reality you could say always possible but not as sure as what you were seeing from those seats: the two horses dragging the carcass of the killed bull, not vivid enough for you to talk of the trailing blood nearly instantly diluted by the rain and muddy earth, but still there had been the killing and that was the necessary moment and as with the automobile races there was a certain dissatisfaction in none of the matadors coming close to being sent to the next world or at the very least the hospital. They were in truth too incompetent as performers to risk being gored and they even avoided a sprain or ache as a result of tumbling in the slime underfoot.

Only in scrupulous memory do I realize how few people were attending and yet that has no consequence as I try to find what my father had to say as we sat there and then after as we found ourselves on the way back to the hotel and the bar where he sat and sat.

We had been together all afternoon and not a sentence of conversation remains. It is possible my sister retains some glimmer of memory of what might have been said or she could imagine he asked where she was going after we had left Mexico City and would she be coming Upstate after she got back and she would be saying she had to prepare for teaching as this was the first or second year of her teaching and there was just so many things to do and he would nod his head and no questions as it all seemed just not of the moment on the bench high up there with no words spoken even as the boy came back a third time with the last beers and Dad went off to find the toilet and I sat conscious of the empty place and what could I say to my sister?

A book is written but parts of it can be discovered elsewhere and become part of the book. DIPTYCH BEFORE DYING went through a number of versions and one evening I was reading three letters my mother had saved from the first years of their marriage and which came to me upon their disappearance. Those three letters sent from Philadelphia, Baltimore and Boston were written and then saved in the years before my birth.

A fourth letter from late in 1945 when I was 14 months old is of interest and provides a voice for this voiceless man sitting in the bullring, in the rain.

HEAD: THE STEVENS Chicago.

FRIDAY NITE 12/28/45

Dearest Darling

Here I am in Chicago. From what Billy said you can give it back to the Indians.

We left New York 5.30 on The Century with the two big bosses L.A.T. & J.P.M. and Ed Gazda the asst. to the Mgr of Sales. We had a nice trip up until 11.30 PM until they told me to look for Ed. Well I looked and looked and walked half way to Chicago but ("I could not find him") he had a girlfriend. We were pretty well out when we "decided to eat." To fool me LAT ordered 4 "Steak dinners" and what a steak the size of our plate the one Tom gave you for Thanksgiving. We had 4 steaks and only three 3 people to eat them. So so LAT and I left the fourth dinner Ed being with the girl friend. I did not mind that one bit. By the way the Bill came to 13.45 for our 3 dinners.

See page 2

(2)

Then we went back to LAT and JPM Room. We all had "double rooms." LAT had a bottle of Rye Scotch and Bourbon. We all three had a double or triple drinks of Rye. It was so much .... on account of what you told me "Watch out." After I finished mine LAT said what's wrong with you Hugh didn't you feel that one? I said what one so he said My gosh what a man. So I had to have another one. I downed that and no feel--- I could of drank all nite and would not felt the effects. We kept that up until about 12.30 AM not waiting for EJG to come back. I finally went to bed. My gosh I cant tell you how much I missed you even though you do not kiss me good nite I could not sleep. I tossed and tossed I was on the upper berth in the room since I knew JG could not make it. When he came in I pretended I was asleep and all he said was What axxxxxxx I was all she was out for was a lot drinks and nothing else. I could of told him that at the beginning "wrong." Remind me to tell you about the morning shaving etc. We arrived in Chicago at 9.45 AM and about 30 min late. We were staying at the place.

(3)

We got to the office OK had a meeting until 1.00PM and then to the Palmer Hotel for lunch. The lunch for 6 men came to 9.35 with 1.65 tip. On the way down I met J McAvery? He was asking for you. We got….. at 2.30 and quit at 5.30 then we were on our own we thought this until we got to our rooms to wash up and clean our shoes etc. when LAT called our room and said there was a meeting up in his room—"drinks" 15 fellows polishing off 3 Ryes 2 scotches and 2 Bourbons then we went down to dinner about 8.30 PM. We went to a place here there was music "etc" I had lake trout and was that good. I had about 7 Seagrams V.O. & Soda before I had the blame dinner. I could not taste one drop. After the dinner went to some place after having a couple at the bar. I mailed a card to Tom from me about trip believe all the girls names… Harold really meant what he said. I left after they were all set since I did not have What do you call them"? We were about 3 miles away from the hotel but I got back…… since I am writing you this.

You can never tell me how much you love me and all that because I love you one H—l of a lot.

(4)

I think more of your little finger than I do of all the loose girls in fact all of the rest of the girls in the world I hope you realize that darling because I am really sick to my insides when I left home thru no fault of mine. I guess you will never understand slips. Why tell too much. I (SMUDGED) never did put anything in writing why start now. All I can say is what I put at the top of this page.

Well Darling guess I will have to stop since it is the last piece of paper in the room.

All the love
Hugh

W.R. is coming in?

Eduardo does not intrude, even in memory. How to indicate the length of our sitting there, with the empty place between us and down in the arena the Pepsi bottle reappeared and made a complete circle of the arena, this time being drawn by a few more guys and with it seemed a few pushing from behind.

And we sat. Could one evoke the cliché of lost in thought but before we were taken for that ride Dad reappeared. He was smoking a cigarette and had a bottle of beer in hand. He was talking, I met a guy, you wouldn't believe it from Brooklyn. The small world he said and I said it is a small world but it was a pretty big place as he was from some part of Brooklyn I didn't know and he didn't really know where Willoughby Avenue was and I didn't go down that road with him, an old fellow like me but maybe not as old, he said, he was here with his wife and his daughter. The daughter had gotten sick and the wife didn't like the shopping as much as out in Acapulco where they had been before and they were going back there on Monday and I told him we were going back to New York on Tuesday and he asked where we were going and I said Upstate and he said he used to go Upstate but really Upstate and I didn't know the place he named . . . but what a small world and I wanted to tell him about going up to . . . but suddenly I couldn't remember the place I drove Nanny and the girls to in the summer, I just couldn't remember it and he didn't want to know so I said I hope the rest of the trip will be okay, did I miss anything?

There was no answer as we didn't really know what we were watching but as it could be said, *you'se* pay your money and you take your chances and Eduardo had offered no guidance in the matter which was okay as what could he possibly say and then Dad said, Gertrude Newman. She must be dead by now. Maybe she isn't.

The rain neither lessened nor got stronger, the day did not get brighter or darker though it felt warmer in a cloying sort of itchy way, but the weather was just a way for the name—Gertrude Newman—to fall into our sitting there, and that is all it did.

When I had gone to Wisconsin to help with their move back to Upstate instead of going to Patchogue, there was a moment in the basement in Grandview Avenue in Menasha as I was moving a pile of photo albums and was looking at the black and white pictures, many of which had a dark full head of hair representation of the bald man who came down the stairs saying, I see you have found the past, no one is interested in any of that, it is from before you were born, before I even met your mother . . .

There was one photograph by itself with a penciled name on the back. Gertrude Newman. Dad said, I think she died.

Gertrude Newman, remember I showed you that picture, I said, but he shook his head no and I could feel a sort of aggressive silence or it might only have been my understanding and then I mentioned, you mean Pine Bush, where you drove Nanny to along with Pat and her mother.

That was the place I should have said but that was all back then, so far back then.

When you are in places like this bullring you forget for much of it where you are and suddenly it seemed, we seemed, so alone, so cut off, such an island midst all the empty seats . . . and there was no way to move, really and there was no more beer to be drank and gradually you get used to the misty sort of rain and something going on *down there* though by now I— and I can only speak for myself—had lost track of how many bulls we had seen killed as none were pardoned, I am pretty sure of that, but in the forgetfulness of so much of the unfamiliar, the one thing that did not happen was the wave of sound encased in the word OLÉ, as the bull passed by the cape which moved in a graceful gesture as the toreador turned and allowed the bull to pass again and turning, again . . .

People did seem to be moving for the exits but we sat inside *you pays your money* so you might as well be there until the show comes to an end. However, Deirdre suggested we leave and say we had been to the very end which in a sense we had come to the end of our time there seeing a bullfight and I am sure we can read about it back in the hotel or at home and who's to know one way or another, it is not as if we know what we are seeing or doing, right now.

Dad did not seem to hear the excuse and still had beer in his bottle and was looking about for the boy with one possibly for the road, though it would be more comfortable back in the hotel, and we would not be in the arena where Gertrude Newman had appeared for ever so a brief moment, as I would imagine happened to cross my father's mind but I was not sure as he was not a person to talk about the past. He existed in the immediate moment: a moment calling for one more for the road and why can't we have one for the road and then we can get a cab back to the hotel.

Enough and the boy did appear with two beers. Dad gave him a five-dollar bill and the boy did not argue. You should not have given him American money, I was saying, and he was saying, is there something wrong with American money and the boy didn't argue with me, didn't he, and took it, happy I am sure, people here take American money all the time, it's easier that way for everyone, really, didn't they take American money in Canada, and I didn't argue with him even though the American dollar was worth, back then a lot more than the Canadian dollar, but I just wanted to be gone from here at the moment.

I was stuck right there, sitting, bottle of beer to the lips, the two empty bottles between my legs, careful not to tip them, sending them rolling and the heads turning to see where the bottles were coming from, and the snap of head back forward as who wants to argue with people like that...

It doesn't matter, Deirdre is saying and we'll be out of here soon and I want a warm shower, I'm not going to get a cold after sitting in the rain all afternoon as I don't want to think about going down to Yucatan with a cold and not feeling good.

But at such a moment—and there is no way to avoid the reality of where these words are being found—the distraction of a moment ago to look to see what emails had arrived:

> Dear Thomas
> Ddogan died in his sleep on Sunday night. We are
>   going home today. I may be back on Sunday
> le gach deaghui
>   Nuala

(Nuala is 61 and her husband is a few years older. She has to fly from South Bend, Indiana, to Dublin.)

And you get the feeling it is time to be going and Dad is still working on the rest of the beer and says he doesn't want to throw up in the cab if you rush me and what's the hurry, we've been here all afternoon and you want to be rushing. Finish what you got in the bottle and let me alone for a moment...

Deirdre stands and says she will take a little walk about and be back and I hope you will be ready to leave. I'm just tired of sitting.

How can I convince you of the descended silence though there had been only that condition for the longest time and since neither of us could even begin to describe what we're seeing and we couldn't talk about the trip to Newfoundland I had thought to mention maybe now was the time to think about going to Ireland next spring as I was going down to Virginia for a month at a sort of colony that was just getting on its feet thanks to a nice letter from Annie Dillard and I also think George Garrett who wanted me to be away from Upstate, as they knew my mother had died and I had left New York City.

But I don't know who this you might be. And there is the possibility my reader might feel excluded for some reason and how do I go about . . .

Are you ready, Dad asks and is standing and he realizes there is now no one sitting behind us and we really are these two human islands and it is time to get going . . .

Let's just wait a moment until Deirdre gets back.

Think of it as a seventh inning stretch. I wonder if they have that idea here like they had at Yankee Stadium, remember you used to come with me to Yankee Stadium, we had those seats right there on the first base line, just over from home plate, from the Can Company, when they had the box, I don't think they had it anymore . . . You know I pitched in Ebbets Field?—a question requiring no answer and even if I had asked how did you come to pitch in Ebbets Field the answer was always it's a long story and no one wants to know all that stuff anymore and so he never did tell me or us how he pitched in Ebbets Field and now no one knows what he or I would be talking about, even back then in that bullring, Ebbets Field was one of those names showing up in the DO YOU REMEMBER column in a local newspaper when it didn't have a sewer department report to run, while the chill came up through the palms of my hands pressed down on the cement bench on which we were again sitting and when Deirdre returned I was up on my feet and she held

Dad under his right arm to make sure he didn't fall front or back and she was sure of her grip and he went along like a stung little boy, a transformation not pleasant and I want to have him die right there and then: Dad, my father and father and my father and it must be so sad for you the way it happened with you all on vacation like that and the mess though the American embassy was wonderful and Deirdre said she had to write to—do you remember the name of the nice consul or whoever it was . . . and do you remember he told us this was one of the easiest of these sorts of things as sometimes he had to go to remote places and there was no refrigeration and he had to take possession—that's the legal phrase for it—of the deceased passport, remains, possessions and all the rest of the stuff.

But now, the taxi driver gestured to use Dad's cigarette to light his own and we were soon back in the hotel.

Dad didn't want to go up to the room to change out of his wet clothes as Deirdre suggested.

I know what I want but if you have to go up to your room go ahead. I trailed behind him and we were back in the bar to the left as you came into the room with him back to the door and me watching this time the people coming and going and not seeing any blonde girls or anyone . . .

Did I recognize the waiter from before or did he recognize me or did he recognize Dad who slapped a five US dollar bill on the little round table: *Si Señor!*—neither of us could read his name on the tag on his red uniform shirt yet there seemed to be some sort of intimacy, that fake intimacy bars always create and it seemed we knew this guy for all eternity or rather Dad had known him for all eternity, as he had the knack coming from somewhere or other and probably came with being able to say *gin mill* and Dad was saying to me, what's his name has been to New York and even to Brooklyn but he didn't like it much and I told him I knew what he was saying and I don't go there myself, there is no one there anymore and only the dead are there and they ain't really even in Brooklyn anymore as some are out on Long Island, but I couldn't tell him the truth that when we all left Brooklyn it was more like Brooklyn had left us and people still go there and they are always going back but for guys like the waiter, they got so many Spanish speaking people there now, but who knows really . . .

Dad's voice just goes away and while I am still sitting there and the beer in front of me is finished and Dad is waiting for the waiter to come back—we can hear him laughing—or I can hear him laughing across the room and saying things loudly in Spanish—his English is spoken very softly, as an accommodation to the two of us and more out of some respect for Dad who is an older man—so, I tell Dad I am going to go for a walk and we will see what to do about tomorrow which is our last day before the day we go back and Deirdre is going away also tomorrow down to Yucatan and Dad says, tell me this tomorrow.

I find myself walking around in the hotel. I do not see Eduardo and take to walking along the corridors and going up the actual staircases and not using the elevators . . . the carpeted corridors are long and have tables at the ends near where the elevators load and unload and chairs and on the lower floors plants are being grown from large pots but there are no plants as you go up to the higher floors and the tables and chairs disappear and while I mostly do not believe in novels that transcribe the thoughts of characters at such moments—as it all seems just too convenient, if you get my drift, there were some thoughts crossing and re-crossing so I was forced back into the end of the year 1972. Of course that was walking along the halls and then the stairs and looking down the stairs, all the way to the bottom but not really as . . .

And I took myself to the room and there noted more things from before we went to Newfoundland starting with a holy card as they were called or a Mass Card or Remembrance Card which was taped to the inside page of my passport.

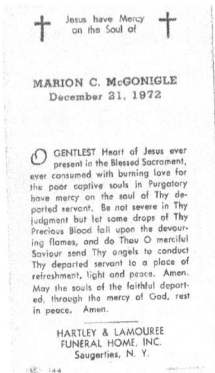

Of course, I did not leave Dad in that bar. He did not have the key to the room as I remembered when I was thinking in the room so had to go down to the bar and bring him back.

Please accept that he had put on the little table in front of him next to the bottle of *cerveza* his ticket from the other day.

Why did we go here, he asked me.

Deirdre thought it would be interesting. We could see the whole city.

Why would anyone want to do that? I never took you up the Empire State building. I don't know what it is that people want to look out at a whole city as they say. You really can't see anything. It's all just a blur.

You seemed to enjoy yourself.

Why would you think that? Your mother wasn't with us.

The waiter was over to the table and bringing back a bottle of beer for me.

We shall be closing soon, Señor, he is saying and Dad is not listening and I am repeating what the guy said and Dad is saying, I can hear perfectly and I am not closing up the bar, he IS and he can close me up inside of it for all I care.

That is not about to happen and you know that.

I don't care anymore for any of this. I want another beer.

The waiter probably knowing what was being said brought another beer even saying, As you say: on the house and good night.

We were both struck by the necessary silence. I knew he was about to say, I miss your mother so much, just so much. And I would have to reply, I understand and he would say, I don't think you can, it has never happened to you and you were always away, I was always with her and she told me, so many times, you were there for me when that family of yours and my family—no one came to visit when I was so sick after Deirdre was born: that mother of yours she said to me and I knew what she meant and I didn't say anything as what could I say. I would want to talk about Lois or about Melinda or Lucja or Barbara and he would look at me like I was reading from a phonebook and I probably knew or I would like to think at this distance from that moment in the hotel bar I did know this but there is no evidence I did know this then and there and knew only I was tired and wanted to go to bed to face our last day before the day we went back up to New York.

We have to be up early to say goodbye to Deirdre . . . she is going on to Yucatan tomorrow . . . why is she leaving us . . . we are going back to Saugerties and she wants to stay on for a little before she has to go back to teach . . .

The explanation all seems beyond the something or other and he says, I don't want to know. I don't want to know, what good is knowing anything?

Let's go upstairs. You've had enough until the morning.

If I had not been such a terrible student, not knowing how to study a foreign language or for that matter how to study anything I would be able here now to write in French the essential distancing from the easy dreary comments about the passage of time . . . and I do know there are no photographs like this of me looking away from . . . Dad is looking the way I could only dream of myself looking and the girl is looking—so long after the fact—into the camera which is taking away her life, little does she know as she is dead within weeks of this photograph and my father only that one time mentioned her name in the basement in Wisconsin—so I could imagine it appearing while we sat in the stadium in the rain . . . in the fountain pen black ink in his tiny script there is her name GERTRUDE NEWMAN.

The elevator, the room and I helped Dad take off his shoes. He just lay on the bed and was asleep. Too often he had said, I learned to close my ears.

I then lay on the other bed and was asleep.

So, in the morning up much too early before even the thought of breakfast and the maybe going out to the Sanborns which was behind the hotel on the ground floor, looking like an American diner, which I guess was its appeal . . . but as I was talking across the lobby of the hotel, Eduardo was asking me if I had enjoyed the anthropology museum yesterday and I had to tell him we had gone to the bullfight with the tickets he had gotten for us and he was saying it all gets confusing and you should excuse me, please, as sometimes, it is not you and the other tourists become one person or one couple: **who has questions, please** but that I have the difficulty of really remembering much of anything from day to days and sometimes it is from hour to hours but I think you are here with your father and he had worked in an office for a very long time if I remember correctly so he would know what I am saying as when you work in an office: days, weeks, months and then years get mixed up and about so the only way you can be remembering a something is by thinking about the first people you met when you started in the office and you remember when one of those first people dies from that time, if you are in a place for a very long time, the way your father was, am I not right, and you mark other events by these events—

But Eduardo, then, took it all away and said: you are probably too young to know what I am talking about and hearing me say it of course marks me out as one of those people who your ears are immune to and while you will run into certain problems trying to remember this man you met in Mexico City, when you were there with your father, you will remember someone said you are too young to really understand what he is saying . . . which calls for a change of the topic of this conversation and you are not yet of the age—there he goes again or there I go—you remember conversations based on topics or events of the day and while I am not much interested in the events of the day, as they call those things that happen in newspapers or on the television, I will say the Anthropology Museum is interesting and while I don't go there to renew that acquaintanceship I do hear from tourists is that it is very . . .

And people are always surprised they find little children sound asleep under pieces of art or inside pieces of art and no one seems to be worried by this and what am I to do as a foreigner who does not speak Spanish, they always say they say and I tell them these children come with parents who have found themselves in Mexico City and are tired and are walking about the museum—which is free on whatever day you visited, when they charge admission you don't see the babies asleep—and which is said to belong to them and the people go and find themselves or a trace of themselves—

Sometimes I think since I work so much with people who are not Mexican I am not Mexican anymore. It is not a good feeling to have when you only look at the city from the eyes of people who are not from here and you only see what they see as that is all they bring to you: the pleasures or the problems they have run into and are only too happy—at great length—to tell me all about what they liked and what they did not like as if I was in charge of a lottery in which certain places rose and fell according to the reactions of foreign people.

For some reason, Eduardo suddenly asked if I minded coming along with him as he had to go to the kitchen to get the rest of his little breakfast which they make up for him and which I still call my breakfast though I am still eating at it, with discretion, at the time of lunch when our guests bring me their first offerings of the day and it is my position to receive and I am not to have a sign I can place on my desk excusing my absence due to lunch of some other natural calling.

There is always a hidden world to add a glamour to our journey, Eduardo says, as he takes me down a corridor I had not seen before and then down a flight of stairs and another flight of stairs as if walking into a black and white movie with the sound removed as no one was speaking as we passed many people wearing various uniforms of their office in the hotel and one could tell those who were not so uniformed so I assumed they were delivering and returning from delivering whatever it is a large hotel requires and then at a sudden turn to the left and a shoved open door Eduardo was collecting a small tray covered with a white linen napkin.

It seemed as if he was collecting a sort of secular version of the chalice and bread and curates of water and wine for a Mass. You noticed as we were walking here there are no signs directing anyone about as it often happens young American women come here searching for adventures—and I am too discreet to tell you the nasty details of those searches but our young men are not so silent in this matter and if you had access to the Spanish language you would hear tales to curl your despair: I did not know the depth of the need and the neglect inflicted upon the women of the United States and which can only be filled—in truth like a little boy trying to fill in the ocean with one tiny toy shovel of sand at a time as in the story asked of a boy in the famous story who was carefully moving a toy shovelful of sand from his brightly colored bucket and carrying it ever so carefully—the shovel and then dumping the sand into the ocean:

Q= What are you doing?
A= Filling up the ocean.

In the brevity of the stepping into the kitchen only the impression of very many people doing things to meat hanging from the ceiling . . . carcasses and blood dripping into containers arranged under the gaping wounds.

I saw nothing more and Eduardo was walking rather slowly back to his office: you can only imagine what they must be wanting when they venture down into this part of the hotel. We have supplied no guards as they only attract more of them looking for something not in their lives.

Suddenly, Eduardo stops himself: why should I talk about something like that? What are we doing, what am I doing? All this is just too ordinary.

Let us return.

With no taking of a breather . . . Eduardo starts in again: did you enjoy the Anthropology Museum? and I have to remind him he had already asked me the question, I thought, but as with everything, I was not sure any more about anything and while I am sure he did ask I was wondering why he was asking me the question again when he could have been asking if we had been to the *Ballet Folklorico* in that wedding cake building across the street and Eduardo was saying one of the advantages among the very few: I do not have to go to such displays and while I might consider going to it if I was in New York City for the very fitful pleasures it might offer and as an adjunct to one's sense of the ironic, since of course I have now appeared in these pages to wrestle with the three Mexicans you have actually talked with—in the flesh, if I may resort to that predestined cliché: Elena Poniatowska, Carlos Fuentes and Oscar Gutman and while you would want me only to fall into words about Fuentes whose *Terra Nostra* caught you in Istanbul in October of 1985—Elena had crossed your journey in 1980 in New York at about the same time Oscar was there finding lines and colors to be put on to paper and canvas . . . but you are hinting always at the dark abyss at the edge of a photograph that finds its way to the page not in any admission of the failure of words as there are plenty of them as you can well see and read if I may be so bold.

A terrible convention all of this business about when is this all taking place?

Right here.

Right here.

That black space beyond the railing . . . and in 2012 as in 1985 and in 1984 I had taken the public ferry up the Golden Horn from the little station near the Galata Bridge to walk up the twisting path of the cemetery below Eyup—you get off at the station before the destination and then walk to sit at the Pierre Loti Café and reading in *Terra Nostra*—**Incredible the first animal that dreamed of another animal** before going on to eventually walk the walls and into the thought of what can really be lost with no memorials to the loss other than melancholic words as are these for that moment, you, Eduardo, call up and if only I could remember your last name and thanks to your children's interest in modern communications would find you in the electronic universe and I would fly down to Mexico City with the same spirit as in 1973 ...

A MOMENT PLEASE. Thank you for your patience as you bear with me as I went away from these moments with Eduardo, leaving my father sleeping up in his room and while Eduardo did not tell me much about the convent across the park that had been turned into a hotel and bar: *we kicked the nuns out years ago and imported the whores to decorate the tables with their slack jaws and shifty tits . . .*

But in the afternoon they are not visible and I haul out my notebook and add lines to previous lines and dread the going back to the hotel and aware: haven't we been to this moment already during these days?

    a - the fingernail of the priest's thumb was broken as he placed the communion wafer on my tongue.
    b - I read four books before I went to college: *A Portrait of the Artist as a Young Man, Look Homeward, Angel, Desire under the Elms, All Quiet on the Western Front*
    c - I knew three poems: I Have a Rendezvous with Death, A Prayer of a Soldier in France, In Flanders Field
    d - miserably happy
    e - the overwhelming majority of guide books are written by hacks who have been fired from TIME Magazine and for people who have not the intelligence to be able to read TIME Magazine.

ENOUGH, please, Eduardo said upon my return to the hotel as he caught me before I could go up to the room. It is wise to be cautious of the indulgence of your potential reader who by now has become used to your digressions yet is waiting for that something to take away with him or her as a memory of this experience.

And I am not some sort of butterfly collector, with net, snatching you from the air through which you move. Far from being caught I stopped you in your tracks with what you must realize is a fatal lurch on your part, the usual retreat into you alone being able to read what you have been composing against the simple fact that who really cares?

While it is true my sister has no interest in revisiting the past: why go back through **all of that** I have been trying to find a way to implicate the interested reader in what is always going away, as my father and I sat at the bullfight, as we went from cantina to cantina to hotel bar and then to museum and then out to see Teotihuacan.

—A LETTER—

Postmark June 3, 1941   THE BENJAMIN FRANKLIN
Chestnut at Ninth Street
PHILADELPHIA.

First Nite away from the
Dearest sweetest wife.

Dearest Marion

Here I am away from you, and I would be telling no lie if I say it is rather................not having you here with me. The trip down was very nice Pullman all the way. Taxi to Hotel. Best Hotel. 4.00 a day nice eats, no drink. Turned down some this afternoon and evening. Mr Moran on the wagon drat him. I don't mind.

I am off to see Kitty Van Meter and Uncle Dick so could you tell

mother. Will try to write you from Baltimore tomorrow nite. If not don't be angry.
                    Hope you can read this writing
                            All my love and more
                                    Hugh
Do you love me? I do

                —A SECOND LETTER—

                THE EMERSON
                A Robt R. Meyer Hotel Baltimore and Calvert Sts.
                Baltimore, MD.

Postmarked June 4, 1941

                2nd Day away from the sweetest girl & Wife a guy
                    ever or would want to have

Dearest Marion
    Pardon the pencil. I am in a hurry to send this so you will receive it Thursday.
Left Philadelphia today Wednesday and got here after 6.00. Going to office tomorrow. Will get the train about 5.00 o'clcok and be home about 10.00 Thursday. Do you miss me? Everything goes what I said in the first letter will be glad to be home with you.
    Went to see the folks in Phil last nite. Tell mother everyone is fine.
        So long for now
                Lots of love and that's all of it
                Hughie.

This morning Eduardo was wearing his left arm in a sling of dark blue material. You had not noticed this detail as you had been reading about Eduardo as it had not been noted in the sentences but he was saying if that is all that remains of me in your mind I will be quite happy or should I admit to being contented by this detail . . .

the guy in the hotel we talked to who had his arm in a sling . . .

I have been waiting for you to be curious about the "extreme" details of my work, my position in the hotel, which is surely more than a person who fetches—good pat on the head dog doing his temporary master's bidding—fetching tickets to doings and comings and places . . . I will not indeed be telling you of kissing children as that is a much too of an emotional scene and well displayed in *Bunny Lake Is Missing* however there are destroyed pets: cats, dogs, birds, rodents, insects even as people travel with the oddest of companions . . . can anyone ever forget the servant dropping into the roaring stove the dead bird of the professor in *The Blue Angel* and the devastation that sweeps across his face—but snakes will not be alluded to as none has been destroyed while staying with our guests.

Of course I might talk of a couple caught in the extreme physical attachment from which the man is unable to withdraw due to the sudden frozen grasping nature of the female's body: a relic of adolescent fantasy to be sure but I do know you want to know: what happens when you find a dead body in a room?

Of course, in this city a dead body is like a demanding hand of the law arriving long before the full embodiment of the law with the necessary crossing of his palm with folding paper money always to be discovered on the floor of the room to be explained away.

The Mexican dead we sweep as with a broom from the hotel. Americans have to be attended to by someone from the embassy and all they are really concerned with is the American passport: that sacred thing at least to them. The actual "remains"—that is another story—and every time the American official comes one can see the reality of any one person's insignificance . . . how this death has taken this man away from the pleasures of picking his nose or fucking the secretary, or being bent over the desk while his superior relieves himself . . . just a royal pain in the ass, if you may excuse the poverty of my language, these young men and now even women come to check up and claim the passport—the women are more masculine than one might . . . they always seem to be saying how oblivious they are to the drama of this premature departure and it is always seen as a premature departure otherwise no hotel would admit anyone into its rooms if this was to be a constant peril . . . you should probably be seeing to your father . . . (but I waved that concern away by saying) he is not going to die upstairs or down in the bar where he probably is, having skipped breakfast and later we will go along to this hotel I saw on the plaza in front of the cathedral where you can have a drink on the roof and look down on the plaza . . .

I know the place, Eduardo says, it has no mural so escapes notice from those who come to this country collecting our art by looking at it and comparing it to the illustrated art books and of course they always talk about what is not captured by the camera and which is only accessible by the actual human eye and never have I really heard anyone reveal something they have not studied in the picture histories . . .

But I was telling you of the collecting of the passports of the dead and the disposal of any connection between the dead and the room in which the deceased was found and the hotel containing the room.

Never has a survivor come to inquire after their dead. They are so gullible, so complacent, so happy to have the line drawn under the other's life without help from their own hands. I remember none of them as individuals. Each is just a dead man or woman who had to be collected. The room had to be locked for a week after the removal of "the remains." When this happens the cleaning staff and the waiters who served the room had to be changed as a certain smell remained about the room, something that was of course imaginary but no one wanted to serve in that room or clean that room as it was the anteroom to the next world, even if only so temporarily and I was always aware of the shallowness of the gullibility of the staff. Surely those being reassigned to that floor knew something had happened but I guess it was simply they too had to give into some sort of renovation of how to think about their superstitions . . .

I wanted to continue the discussion but Eduardo suggested I see to my father and then your sister is going off, as you said and you should be sure to see her away.

She has no need for me to say goodbye to her, we will be seeing each other soon enough back in New York but you might be right and there is always later . . .

She had no wish to prolong the farewell as she just wanted to be away for the same reasons I had wanted to be away and was there, if you follow what I am trying to say . . .

It had been my suggestion the going to Newfoundland and now Mexico City. If I could detail the reasons I would not have been there, so that was why I am here.

Deirdre had acquired the bus ticket and didn't mind me walking with her to the place beyond the market where the bus was leaving for the south. I was not to stand and watch the bus leave. She didn't want the eyes of the passengers to be looking at me, looking for where she was in the bus and this marking her out for a certain attention. It is best not to betray what you are leaving behind, she had learned traveling by bus in Tunisia and in Libya . . . she had not married while traveling as I had done, she had not brought a husband home to *The States*, as Americans liked to say, as I had brought a wife and of course the first sentence was always the unspoken one: she had married you to get to *The States* . . .

A better traveler than I ever would be, I could admit only later . . . and as I walked back to the hotel I went to the cathedral and remember only the darkness in the far aisles and thinking of Bloom in the church on Westland Row in Dublin . . . an allusion to be frowned upon as one does not like to read of books having been read as one is reading . . . why isn't he out there describing life, life . . . : so okay, the side of the bus was smeared with red mud along the length of it, as what was the point of washing down the buses as they would just get muddy again.

Her pleasing expression and myself turned away toward the cathedral—*down there*— Dad had taken the picture fixing us in the place and while it is only a photograph: shadowing these words as anything can be read into her face and his turned-away eyes are yet aware he is being looked at through the camera's eye.

It seems to have been a gray sort of day as you can see how he is dressed and she is dressed out of respect for where she is. Deirdre had a coffee and Dad and I each had a *cerveza*—did I try to remember the Spanish word for *cold*? . . .Probably letting the waiter know I was trying, trying in what way I did not consider, I know that, now, always know that, **now**: but for then again the waiter was kind and showed respect for our father and with Deirdre sitting there he had carefully arranged glasses, bottles, cup and saucer on the table, smile without a trace of smirk toward me who was waiting for that understanding so I could . . . I heard Dad saying, your mother would like sitting here, she liked to go out, I didn't like going out as I was out in the office or on the train, but she liked going out and we went out more in Menasha, I hope you know that?

We had different experiences of Wisconsin, Deirdre said. I worked one summer in the cheese recycling place, remember? We would get the cheese that had been shipped back by supermarkets and had to unwrap the stuff and cut off the bad bit and put it all in some sort of container as it would get used then for dog and cat food and sometimes reshaped up for people to eat. That was the only job I could get one summer . . . the other summer I worked at the can company in the office in Neenah . . .

And then I said my piece: I taught seventh grade the year I came there with Lilia . . . remember we came by bus from New York, after flying from Dublin. Lilia got a job assembling TV tuners down in Oshkosh and I got a job teaching at the Catholic school in Menasha. She didn't stay long at the factory and went to Oshkosh and took a course and got a job first in the cafeteria and then in the Geography Department where she helped make maps for the husband of the Russian professor and I took two courses and drove back and forth to Oshkosh, back and forth to Oshkosh.

Did you say that guy's name was Silent, Dad suddenly asks.

Who do you mean?

The guy who got us the tickets for the bullfight.

No, it was Eduardo. He has a friend who has the name *Silencio* . . . I couldn't figure out how he got the name either: he talks too much or doesn't speak at all . . . the cat ate his tongue or it just runs away with him.

Not for a moment do I believe you, Deirdre says, and I replied, it doesn't matter one way or the other . . . you have your story of Wisconsin and I have my story of Wisconsin and I was the one who was out in Wisconsin helping them move back East and you had been out there more when they were first there.

I was happy to be away for two Christmases in a row, and it would have been better to have missed four Christmases as I was there the year I came back from Dublin and drove up to Menasha from Beloit for the first time in a snowstorm and remember—still— stopping at the shopping street in Neenah realizing I still had to get to the twin city, and the snow was coming down and I had the feeling I am coming into this town for the first time and my mother and father no longer live in Patchogue, on Long Island, sixty miles from New York City but are now in Wisconsin and not in Neenah where I have stopped and have to go on to Menasha which looks like it is still across a river or some sort of water and finally one is in Menasha which they say is a twin city and the most memorable thing about the town is that it is on Little Lake Butte des Mortes, the place of their exile from the East, from Patchogue, from The City, New York.

You're just being dramatic, Deirdre says. You don't really care what it was really all about: you just want to make it into words, just words. Am I right? She turns to Dad who is looking away, but in reality just looking at the wall about where we are sitting and he starts to stand, wobbles a bit and sits down again.

I want to go back to the hotel.

Let's go back to the hotel, Deirdre says.

The conversation has come to an end. No one gets in the last word which might be a good thing or everything is always is up in the air.

Why didn't we stay at this hotel, Dad asks as we are walking back to the Del Prado.

The travel agent put us into the one where we are staying. It is fine enough.

I guess so. It is big enough. I used to travel for the can company all the time.

I know. What happened?

They stopped sending me places. And I didn't like being away from your mother.

Of course we could all be found out, three Americans walking along a crowded street in Mexico City, talking English about what was of course not right around us at the moment though Dad never looked into windows and Deirdre was not one to look in windows and I was looking at the faces passing by and never one to be recognized or to be recognized by. Millions of people and not a single one of them had a name we could say: I know a person, I have this friend living in, giving some street, in Mexico City and Eduardo looking at us, I don't know every street in the city but you can find it on the map and why don't you go to look for your friend, but there was no such name and we walking along the street, by the bank with the gunslingers in front walking back and forth with heel of hand on the back of the holstered pistols: only one gun at hip and not two as I thought I saw on the other day . . . and Deirdre was asking why did you notice something like that, what does it tell a person about Mexico City or really anything: it is just something you saw and people always look at you when you say I have been . . . And there is a pause and eventually: what was it like and you tell them as you say you noticed the bank guards walk back and forth in front of the bank with gun slung low on the hip as if waiting for a guy to attempt to draw a gun on them and then rush the bank, yet I will give you credit for not asking now what Tunisia was like and what was it like to be there for two years and why did you decide to stay when you were presented with the challenge: do you really want to stay in Tunisia for the next two years and you didn't ask me what reasons I gave as we did have to give reasons for why we wanted to stay in Tunisia as the process was called self-assessment, self-judgment, self-deciding what to do as opposed to what I think you had which was *they* decided who was to go and who was not to go and they used, did you say, a very pernicious method to identify: each "volunteer" had to list five people who you thought should go to Turkey and five people who you thought should not go to Turkey.

This was a very clever way of avoiding one person having to decided who should go and who should not go and I remember I told Deirdre there was an interview with a psychologist and he told me I had an answer for every question he asked but he was not sure my answers were exactly answers as opposed to what I had thought was the answer expected from me with the view to going to Turkey. I did not reply to him and it made it harder as he was trying to provoke me into something or other and I was not about to allow it.

These self-assessment tests, these personality tests were so patently obvious you could construct any personality you wanted if you stepped back a moment from them and decided who you were for the moment.

In any event, as is said in novels and sometimes even in life: I broke my knee so did not go to Turkey as a volunteer and received workman's compensation since I was a worker unable to work.

Naturally, it is possible to believe this conversation did not happen as we walked back to the hotel and Deirdre stopped to buy postcards and I had bought one of two postcards and probably sent one to Melinda, but I am not sure of it, as she had not yet ascended to the role of the permanent disappointment replacing her original situation as muse which had been far more hopeful but always compromised by the genuine possibility: the result of her inspiration would be rotten on the vine before it had been . . .

—LETTER ONE—

HOTEL STATLER BOSTON
Park Square at Arlington Street
Monday Nite
(Postmarked August 4, 1941)

Dearest Marion

Gee its lonesome. What will it be tomorrow if I am so now.

Arrived 9.00 PM. Had a swell dinner on the train. The prices Oh my 2.00 got just about 10 small potato balls and steak.

Thought I'd drop this tonite so you can get it Tuesday. Going to call

my aunt and see if they are home.
    Will let you know when I will be home.
            All my love and ore if possible
            Hugh.

—LETTER TWO—

HOTEL STATLER BOSTON
(Postmarked August 5, 1941)

    Tuesday
    Very Lonesome

[up in corner]: I will try to get the 3.00 . . . train so to be in NY 8.00. I'll come home you don't have to meet me.

Dearest Marion

    Do you know what today is I love you more and more than before.
    Back from the office and whata day hot. I was wet all day outside not inside. Not a drink so far going to try and not drink all the time I'm away. Oh I forgot had a bottle of beer for my dinner last night. Got up at 7.30 AM took a shower, then down to breakfast. The hotel gives you the morning paper for nothing then went for a walk and then the subway to South Station. Trolley cars underground for 2 stations then a subway for 2 more stations Ten 10cents fare up here got to office about 10.00 oclock they start at 8.15 did they rib me for coming so late how should I know they start so early I am now going to take a shower and then go out to have dinner. You know dear it not the same eating by myself without you to make face at. I will go over to see Aunt Ellen tonite I called last nite and told them I am going. Tell Mother to drop her a line, she said she wrote last.
    Will close with all my love to the sweetest wife a guy ever had. How are you feeling? I'll be home.
            All my love
            Hugh.

Naturally, Eduardo stopped me for possibly the last time and wished me and your father a good journey home to The States . . . one learns, he adds quickly, never do I wish to see you upon your return as I well know the process of forgetting that will inevitably occur upon your return to where ever it was you had come from down to Mexico City and to which you return and in some way you are already back in that place as when a person goes away there is always the initial excitement of the leave-taking, the going and while there is a brief parenthesis of doubt as to why ever am I going away that is easily swept away in the actual going and now there is the mirror of a mental burp you could say: why did I ever go away and yet I did go away and there is the landing and the customs in New York is just so arbitrary: the pleasures the guards of your country take in descending on the least likely of suspects and never finding anything of course, as the real gangsters have it all arranged ahead of time, when it comes to the real stuff that must be got into the country, but you always feel the burden of return and the voice: Welcome to the United States, and there you are with your bags, a little heavy you admit and your father needs to use the toilet after holding it in as is said during the flight as he was afraid to stand and use the facility on the plane and you dreaded him either having an accident or the weaving to the toilet and the bumping into passengers, and here you are and you just want to get to the car over there in the EXTENDED PARKING LOT, and he has to use the toilet and you want to be getting going as you want to get Upstate, is it not, where you come from: Upstate from New York City and the drive is not pleasant as there is always too much traffic and you really don't look forward to being up there again and are already planning when you can leave and you have in your mind: left already yet you need to go through the form of being back home from your week in Mexico City and I have now become a name attached to that phrase, a very helpful guy in the hotel who got us the tickets for the bullfight and got us the car to take us to the pyramids as you still can't say the Mexican name for where you have been and you take out of the little box the silver necklace: a skeleton of a fish hanging from a silver chain and gradually it will be the only object to commemorate your week in Mexico City. Of course in mind I remember we do have some postcards and there are photographs in the Sure Shot or is Easy Shot Pocket Camera and later they will be developed and as they are in color, at the edges, as the years go by, a yellow stain begins to appear and eventually this stain will wipe away the image as surely as time . . . to echo a poet, I think, though Silencio is better at making those connections but he does not speak English and you can only hope to one day see his words translated into English or imagine what he might be saying in Spanish so you can hear it in English far from this place both in space and time as the newspapers are likely to say.

You are wondering what will remain of the week and while there is no real telling: the bullfight, the trip to see the past heaped up in stone so as to imagine the ripping of a living heart out of the chest of a young man and then a young woman and the gruesome washing in the blood: how we enjoy the thought of that—I can assure you . . . but I am not supposed to partake of these thoughts, so ordinary.

You are wishing to see what I carry in my little case from home to work and you would find one of those picture novels . . . with the bubbles of conversation above the distressed faces and the ecstatic faces: there is always hanky-panky—is that the word—there is a body face down with a pool of blood and our women in black and a young taller, fair woman looking away and you discover the man in a few more panels and then you find them lying under a sheet pulled up to their chins knowing one of them is going to have that sheet pulled over their face.

It matters little whether it is the man or the woman who is to be extinguished . . . I read to pass the time . . . it is in the actual sentences and the what is to happen next keeping me turning the pages and that is how it really is for most people, as you well know: that getting lost in a book, as is said— when I went to New York and when I went to London and when I went to Paris I relied on only the tiny map they give you at the hotel and even that I always seemed to lose.

The point of going away is to get lost, I told myself, and tried to live by that thought in spite of knowing I had only had two weeks in those cities but two weeks is more than enough to last a lifetime as what is left over . . . of course I knew those cities better than most as I had gotten lost in the reading about them though please don't ask me to attach authors and titles to my understanding: Silencio has that advantage over me and nearly everyone I know: he has been to every city in the world and has never left Mexico City as why should one actually go to those other places—they inevitably have to disappoint since one remembers only details and usually details as mundane as the absence of toilet paper in a place where one would have expected to find such or there was a crying baby or hysterical young man or a rainstorm or a snowstorm or a heat from which there was no relief or a cold one felt could have broken your fingers off.

Silencio was afflicted by the perfection of his method of travel and I confirmed him it with my walks through Paris or London: yes, London where Francis Bacon bought me my own small bottle of champagne: a split for the young one, he said, in that pub called The French Pub, you will one day discover it, he said. All young men of a certain time and place seem to have gone to The French Pub . . . and had a split of champagne placed in front of them at the little table to the right of the bar where Bacon liked to sit. It is Bacon who told me of preferring the photographs from the 19th Century. All the subjects are safely dead and once were so alive. He said he could not help but distrust those who wanted a photograph of himself as really gathering them so they could look at the picture and say: I knew him when he was alive and now he is dead and this photograph only captures the moment of his being alive and there is no way of telling if it is a real likeness as the face changes second to second as the words whip across that façade like tiny razors, he was fond of saying: tiny razors . . . in spite of being Mexican I was a disappointment to Bacon, I must tell you. I was not rough enough, he said, and I knew exactly what he was hoping of me: that I would raise my arm, my left arm, form the hand into a fist and jerking it suddenly as if to rear even further back bring it sharply down but not banging the top of the little table . . . prudence, he said: prudery—not wanting to risk my not replacing the split . . .

Silencio avoids of course all those impossible meetings and even tried to dispute my claim I had been in that pub with Francis Bacon as he had not considered this possibility in his travels about in London . . .

While, you are now growing impatient and must be resuming your own experience of Mexico City and now you have to try to cram as much of it as you can into the remaining day as the next day you leave and already the hours have ticked away and yet you have nothing really to show for the time here, now have you?

I left Eduardo with a wave of the hand and nod of head as he was good on the necessity of sign language at the moment and went to the lobby where midst a sea of arriving and departing luggage I sat myself down and thought as the poet might suggest: which way to the right or to the left going out of the hotel and I went to the left as the right was to walk by the gunslingers in front of the bank and the bookstore with the imported Penguin books and dusty old American books left behind by tourists who had exhausted the books and the exhaustion was so evident in the turned pages as no enjoyment would ever be found in the pages . . .

> The Past is Terrifying, an Abyss;
> All that Enters
> into its Darkness Ceases to
> Exist, nor Did It Ever Exist
>
> A heading in *MIGRATIONS* by
> Milos Tsernianski

At the end of the street was the beginning of some sort of high-speed highway I seem to remember and with such a doubt I stood by the road and tried to think my way into one of those cars but as we had met no one other than Eduardo and his friend Silencio—Mexico City would be pictured in the movies by Buñuel and there had been the movie *The Assassination of Trotsky* directed by Joseph Losey—we didn't find the garden with the punts being rowed about and I was not about to walk into a shop to buy a pick-axe and hear the applause of the critics at the New York Film Festival screening of the movie finally applauding as they knew now we were getting close to the murder of Trotsky and even being Richard Burton, Trotsky was going to have his head split open and MORGAN appeared with a soft boiled egg having its top removed and Morgan alluding to Trotsky and Dwight MacDonald forsaking movie reviewing as the jocular nature of the movie put into suspicion his whole younger years when he was much concerned with the fate of Trotsky...

Not for a moment is anyone going to follow much of this even if it is as they say necessary background to the final arc of the prose taking the reader to:

> I buried my mother yesterday and now it is
> Christmas Eve Upstate in a field behind the house
> on 9W going north out of the town of
> Saugerties—buried not here but on Long Island in
> St Charles Cemetery off Route 110...

I was going to that hotel where I sat for two afternoons in the *Zona Rosa* but there was some sort of meeting in the large room where I had been **at work** at my writing, if it could be called that and even then, I knew, there was something wrong, yet that did not stop me and how awful it was to be just writing and I had tried to ask myself what was the purpose for all this and then there was the reading and while I had not read before that senior year of high school . . . I was not immune to reading but I did not like to read fiction, those made-up stories ending just when they seemed to become interesting yet the sheer lack of power to add to what one had read as so many of the books seemed beyond any claim . . .

A death had sent us on these journeys with no purpose of discovery, with no search for a person who might be of some assistance, a being sent into the future on a quest was to be postponed to another time or to a time not at all.

As I walked on the wide avenue not a comment was made. Not a sudden shove, not a smile, not a look said to be made of daggers . . . no sudden braking of cars at the crossings as I did not cross to the far side of the avenue and this stretch of the avenue was unbroken as far as I was prepared to walk. I was not to cheat death and talk about how dangerous the driving is in Mexico City and we did not see a funeral leaving the cathedral as we had seen in Paris, one time many years later, to violate the space and time of these sentences, long after this journey to Mexico City, but a necessary flaw to allow you to find me on this avenue and the heading back to the hotel and the waiting as that is what had to be endured but we had gone to the *Ballet Folklorico* and seen the "authentic folk tradition as seen in New York City and in all the capitals of Europe" and indeed around the world but the dance routines seemed closer to the opening of the Jackie Gleason Show, a reference revealing far more than . . . (where will the footnote be entered) . . . but in the moment such is but a click away into a search engine and one is dancing with the

June Taylor Dancers, but a kid might be saying: I guess you had to be there and what was the point of being there since none of that stuff remains beyond the words you have found for these lines and you say your father is in the bar waiting for something or other and Eduardo makes a final appearance as he has to leave work a bit early and his assistant who I have never met and did not know he had an assistant is also unavailable so our dear guests are just going to have to amuse themselves based on their own reckoning. It was my pleasure to provide you with the sites of a few memories and I am already just . . . and you have left in some way already for The States and I wish you a good journey. Your sister has already gone so it now just your father and you for the remaining hours, neither of you knowing for sure how many hours are left and that is all to the best: imagine how awful it would be if each and every one of us was constantly aware of what you could name in a countdown mode as you see them at them at the first second, then minutes, then hours then days, then weeks, then months and the years . . .

Dad had gotten the beermats to shape a little shelter closed on three sides and about to place a fifth mat so as to form a mausoleum but he could not get the fifth card to rest as the closing rock and no, I am not making a parody of the Easter story . . .

So much might depends on getting that card exactly placed but I am not the story teller . . .

So, soon back in Saugerties: and yes, I had written down the conversation:

> Hello.
> Tom.
> Dad is that you?
> Yes. Your mother passed away this morning. She was alright; half an hour later she passed away. I don't know what to do.

Did you call Deirdre?

The phone is busy.

I'll call her.

What shall I do?

We'll be up there this afternoon. I'll call you back.

McGonigle residence.

Dad, I called Deirdre, we'll be up there this afternoon.

Okay.

Is the priest there?

Yes.

See you then.

Deirdre, Mom died this morning.

O, no, what are we going to do.

Get Allen to drive you to your apartment. I'll be there between one and two.

I have not seen Lois Alexeevna is a month. What a terrible name for the accident of meeting a girl who says she is related to the Russian writer Andreyev. I insisted on calling her Lois Andreyev as a way to avoid having to say her first name.

Mom is dead. The body: the face is stern, hard, the right eye is tightly closed, the left is as if it were about to open and I would hear her say, AND THEN? I have her nose, my eyes are sunk into my head, her lips. Short stumpy fingers folded one on top of the other. The rosary wrapped as if binding them.

The lid of the casket. Carried the casket up the steps of the church on a hill surrounded by an old cemetery of course the word *Golgotha* as the stones lean drunkenly talking always at three in the morning.

That night I said goodnight to Lois Alexeevna as I lay on the floor of the living room in the house in Saugerties. I made the soundproofing ceiling into the ceiling of the Doge's palace in Venice . . . anything to escape. My mother died at about 9 AM Thursday December 21, 1972. She knew she was going to die since the night before. She did not ask for me and she left no message, she had watched the *Julie Andrews Show*, a musical variety show—I am not sure if she listened to it from the bedroom or was she able to come into the living room where the television was? . . . and she did not, she did not . . . and in the news Harry Truman died on December 26th.

I woke up with a skull next to me on my pillow. I saw later that week the Ingmar Bergman movie *Cries and Whispers* and David Black was telling me: Michelangelo going to the graveyard and putting his arm up the anus of a corpse, along the alimentary canal into the corpse's mouth and he became sick when the tips of his fingers touched the back of the teeth . . .

But in reality, as the prosecuting attorney might say: we were still in Mexico City and while you have taken care of the future, though that rather pathetic aspect of being alive is obvious to anyone who has lingered through these pages, you and your father are still in Mexico City and maybe one last beer in the cantina and again the reminder that the photograph still has not turned up so his hand is forever on the top of the right swinging door as he is preparing to enter the bar, has turned to look at me holding the camera and he says, are you coming in?

On the flight up to New York Dad fell into talking to the woman to his right as he was sitting on the aisle and I was sitting on the other aisle seat next to him, as it were. She gave me her address and phone number and told me she would call or I could call when I got back home as she lives near us somewhere or other.

I do not know what they talked about but the conversation went on for the hours of the flight. Living in a household of women he had often said he learned how to close his ears and listen. People just want you to listen to them but you need to listen in a way that makes sure you . . .

You'll be hearing from me, she said as she walked away and he said, sure thing. He gave her a little wave with his right hand but the meaning was not obvious and I only noted it as I did when we did back up to Saugerties that there was a large envelope from the Irish Tourist Board as we had talked of maybe going to Ireland in the Spring.

Dad sat himself down in *his* chair to the left of the picture window looking across the lawn to 9W and then the mountains in the far distance behind the hill where Judge Cody lived, a nice man, Dad said, he was very kind when your mother . . .

I miss your mother. I was sitting here when . . .

The rest of the story is known only to God.

But there seems to be something heartless about leaving him there as I saw him in that chair as I was taking the train to Washington, D.C., to Richmond, to Charlottesville and then a few days later—was it a week? A phone call saying he had died and they arranged for me to fly up to New York from Charlottesville, via Washington where I stepped across the puddle of blood where someone had fallen and the blood had not been cleaned up. I had to take the bus up to Saugerties and begin waiting. He was not in the house. The ashtray was overflowing on the table next to window where he sat in *his* chair. The envelopes from the Irish Tourist Board had not been opened. There was a fragment of a letter he was writing on the kitchen table.

About the Author

Thomas McGonigle (b. 1944) is a writer, literary and art critic, university professor, and journalist. He has received several awards, including the Notre Dame Review Book Prize (2016). His novel *The Corpse Dream of N. Petkov* was first translated into Bulgarian by Ivanka Tomova for the *Syvremennik* magazine in 1991 and was republished by Ciela Publishing House in 2019. Inspired by the story of Nikola Petkov, a politician and member of the opposition, executed by the Communist regime, McGonigle introduces his readers into the setting of the National Court through the stream of consciousness of Nikola Petkov himself.

McGonigle is also author of the novels *Going to Patchogue* (1992), *St. Patrick's Day: another day in Dublin* (2016), *Party of Pictures* (2023), and *Empty American Letters* (2023). He is a contributor to the *Los Angeles Times*, the *Washington Post, Newsday*, the *Chicago Tribune*, and *The Guardian* in London.

www.ingramcontent.com/pod-product-compliance
Lightning Source LLC
LaVergne TN
LVHW051953060526
838201LV00059B/3627